THE HONORARY JERSEY GIRL

D0104680

To Mark,
with a boha t thanks)
—Al Tuch

the honorary jersey girl

by Albert Tucher

Published by Shotgun Honey, an imprint of Down & Out Books

Shotgun Honey
PO Box 75272
Charleston, WV 25375
www.ShotgunHoney.com

Down & Out Books
3959 Van Dyke Rd, Ste. 265
Lutz, FL 33558
www.DownAndOutBooks.com

Cover Design by Bad Fido.

First Printing 2019

ISBN-10: 1-948235-10-2
ISBN-13: 978-1-948235-10-5

In loving memory of
Albert Tucher (1926-2011) and
Doris Tucher (1925-2012)

THE HONORARY
JERSEY GIRL

1

AGNES RODRIGUES SCANNED the room and wondered what the ten-hour flight had been for. Rosen's restaurant could have passed for Ken's House of Pancakes back home in Hilo. A diner was a diner.

And a red eye was a red eye. Her body was clamoring for coffee. She hoped they served it in New Jersey.

They probably did, because the woman in the corner booth had a carafe in front of her. Her name was Diana Andrews, and changing her mind was the reason for this trip.

Andrews was not exactly beautiful, but her strong cheekbones, stronger nose, and brown eyes with their slightly Asian cast issued a challenge—are you good enough?

For years, Agnes knew, men had paid by the hour to find out. Diana Andrews had been out of that business for years, but Agnes needed this woman for what she was doing now. Andrews ran a company that specialized in personal protection.

Bodyguarding. Agnes thought it might be more harrowing than going behind closed doors with any man who put his money down. Maybe she would get an opportunity ask about that.

Agnes started toward the booth. Andrews looked at her without surprise or concern, but Agnes doubted that this woman ever revealed what she was thinking. Agnes had defended many prostitutes. Hooking taught them the value of a poker face, and for Diana Andrews a knack for giving nothing away probably helped in corporate life.

Heads swiveled to follow Agnes, as she made her way through the breakfast crowd. She knew she issued challenges of her own, starting with the question of her ancestry. She was Hawaii on the hoof. Back home everyone understood that, but here, five thousand miles away, few onlookers would recognize the island mix of Portuguese, Japanese and Filipino genes that produced women like her the way the volcano pumped out lava.

Agnes slid into the booth. The other woman's "don't fuck with me" look would have worked on most people, but Agnes had sat across the table from men who were facing life in prison, and for good reason.

"I usually wait to be invited," said Andrews in the voice Agnes had heard saying no on the phone.

"I don't have that kind of time."

"I told you, I won't do it."

"Get paid to go to Hawaii?"

"I've been to Hawaii."

"That's why I called. You know the territory."

"Hawaii almost killed me. Twice."

Agnes studied the woman. Andrews looked serious.

"Detective Coutinho didn't tell me that part."

"Coutinho talks to defense attorneys?"

"We're not friends, but if he tells me something, I take it to the bank. He admits you're the best in the business. Which impressed me, because I could tell you're not his favorite person."

Andrews ignored the compliment, if that was what it was.

"How did you find me here?" she asked.

"I'm from the Big Island. I know small towns."

"And?"

"It's too early for the office. So I went looking for breakfast, and there aren't many choices."

"I think Drake told you where I would be."

"Drake?"

"Don't play dumb. He's been after me to take this job. Why would that be?"

Agnes felt as if she had just made a rookie mistake in court, and Andrews was the judge who had called her on it.

What does a lawyer do when she doesn't know what to do next? She smiles her most confident smile and stalls.

The morning waitress appeared and set two menus down. Agnes made a mental note to tip the young woman extra for the timely distraction.

"I'll stick with coffee, thanks."

By the time the waitress finished pouring, Agnes had decided on her next move.

A frontal assault.

"My client was acquitted," she said. "He's innocent. I don't mean not guilty. I mean he didn't do it."

No response. Agnes met the woman's eyes. It took some effort.

"Obviously," said Agnes. "I investigated you. You've known some criminal lawyers. In both of your careers."

Andrews didn't deny it.

"So you know it's my job to get up in court and say my clients are innocent. But do you know how many times I believe it?"

Andrews wasn't going to give her a thing, but Agnes went on.

"This time I do, and the police aren't taking it well. It was a cop's wife who was murdered."

Still nothing.

"Somebody took a shot at my client once already. His name is Hank Alves, by the way."

Andrews didn't care.

"I'm sure it was the cops."

"Coutinho doesn't do things that way."

Agnes filed that away. It was interesting that Andrews rose to Coutinho's defense, when he could definitely live without her. It showed a fundamental fairness that Agnes hoped to exploit.

"Tell him and I'll deny it, but I wish they were all like him."

Andrews shook her head.

"I can't do it. For so many reasons."

Diana Andrews knew how to say no. That was another thing prostitutes learned early.

"Thanks for your time," Agnes said.

She slid out of the booth and dropped a ten next to her cup. Andrews was looking down at her menu, as if the conversation had never happened. Agnes turned and headed for the exit.

2

OUTSIDE, SHE PAUSED on the sidewalk and looked across the street. The municipal building in Driscoll housed the police department. For a few minutes she watched the uniformed officers coming and going. They mingled with detectives who didn't need uniforms to look like cops.

It was a scene that she saw every day back home. It made the long trip seen even more futile, and she couldn't allow that. Agnes went into her bag for her cell phone and selected a number that she had recently stored in her contacts.

"Drake," said a male voice in her ear.

"She's not buying it."

"Okay, plan B."

"Are you sure? This is not a boss you want to piss off."

"That's the point. She's the boss, and this is what we do—protect people and get paid for it. There's no good reason to turn this down."

"How is she about being challenged?"

"From me she'll take it. I know when she needs a nudge, and she knows I know."

"She has real issues with Hawaii."

"There are reasons for that, but this is still business."

"Okay. The ball is in your court."

Agnes disconnected and started to look for her car. What had she rented? Probably a Camry. It was what she drove back home.

But when she pressed the button on the key fob, a black Maxima flashed its lights. She couldn't remember a thing about this car that she had already driven a hundred miles.

Talk about distracted. Agnes got in and started driving south to Morristown.

Before booking her room, she had made sure the hotel had a bar. At ten that evening she made her entrance. Heads swiveled, as they always did in the Kohala resorts back home. She tagged a couple of prospects with mental bookmarks and made her way to the bar. As she slid onto a stool, she felt a glare scorching her from the right.

A blonde in her mid-forties occupied the last barstool. Agnes looked back, and Diana Andrews came to mind again. There was no real resemblance, other than the laser-eyed lack of illusions. This woman was a pro, and this was her territory. Agnes didn't know how things worked here, but it wouldn't be unusual for the woman to have a local cop or two on her side.

Agnes signaled the bartender. He came right over. Male bartenders always did.

"Bourbon rocks, and give my friend at the end whatever she's drinking."

The woman shook her head at the bartender and kept glaring. Agnes got up and approached.

"Message received. I'm going to finish me drink and go. So you might as well have one on me."

"I keep a clear head while I'm working."

"Diana says hello."

"I doubt it."

"Okay, she doesn't."

Agnes returned to her seat. On impulse she got her cell phone out and selected a number that was figuring prominently in her *Recents*.

"Diana Andrews."

Agnes wondered whether the woman was in her office at this hour. Andrews was unlikely to tell her.

"Maybe you can tell me how much trouble I'm in."

Agnes explained. Andrews laughed shortly.

"Heather. We used to be friendly enough, but she's pissed at me for getting out of the life while she's still in it. Don't worry about it, but you might want to look for company someplace else."

"It was a bad idea, anyway. I don't know the rules here."

There was a pause.

"Drake will see you at the airport," said Andrews.

"Okay."

Agnes had a feeling that thanks wouldn't be welcome.

"Tomorrow, then," she said.

3

ONE NON-STOP FLIGHT went from Newark to Honolulu each day. When Agnes found her gate the next morning, Drake was already waiting. He got up and shook her hand. Agnes suppressed a smile. She knew he was an ex-SEAL and over thirty, but many people would have mistaken him for a Princeton undergraduate.

A woman joined them. Agnes had noticed her but hadn't connected her with Drake. Agnes realized that someone with bad intentions might make the same mistake, and that was the point.

"This is Tulla Konner," said Drake.

Uh oh, Agnes thought.

There was a reason she had noticed Konner. Once in a while she saw a woman who activated her latent bisexual gene, if there was such a thing. It was often someone like this—six feet tall, with the shoulders of a male athlete tapering to a trim waist and then flaring into womanly hips. The trousers didn't fool Agnes. Put this woman in a skirt and heels, and her legs would cause whiplash injuries in male onlookers.

Her handshake was delicious, just hinting at her strength.

Trust Diana Andrews to hire a woman like this without seeing her as a threat to her dominance.

"Good," said Agnes.

She could see that the two operatives understood her meaning. They made an effective team—one intimidating bodyguard type and one who could blend into the scenery. Usually, the traditional sex roles had things the other way around, but this would work.

"We have a long flight," said Agnes. "I brought the case file, if you want to look at it."

"We don't care what he did."

Okay, so Konner wasn't perfect. Her voice belonged to a petite cheerleader.

"Or didn't do," said Agnes.

"Still doesn't matter."

If her new companions weren't going to take the file off her hands, Agnes knew she would obsess over it some more. She had been reading it again and again, as if there still might be something she hadn't noticed, something that would implicate Don Savage his wife's murder.

They were traveling coach, because Agnes didn't know how she would pay the bill she would run up with Litvinov Associates. She fit well into a coach seat, and Drake would survive, but Tulla Konner's knees would suffer for ten and a half hours. The woman was a professional stoic, and she made no comment.

Agnes did give her the aisle, even though her own bladder was already panicking at the idea of being trapped. Drake had the middle seat.

"About your bill," he said.

"We need to talk about that."

"It's covered."

Agnes turned and looked at him.

"Diana has an angel," said Drake.

"What does that mean?"

"A man who says he owes her. He writes six figure checks without blinking."

"There must be a hell of a story behind that."

"Someday I hope to find out."

"I wasn't sure you could pull this off. Getting her to go along, I mean."

"Well, you helped," said Drake.

"I didn't have that impression."

"Trust me, you did. She said you treated the waitress right. That goes a long way with Diana."

"Oh."

Agnes digested that. It made sense. A lot of people who hired prostitutes thought they had bought the right to treat them like garbage.

"I'm still impressed that you have this influence on her."

"You know why she's president of Litvinov Associates?" said Drake.

"I'll bet there's a story in that too."

"There is. The founder was Roy Litvinov. He hired her for a job. It went bad, and Diana was the only one who came out alive. Roy's widow made her president, but then Bethany thought Diana would just be a figurehead. Diana disagreed, and we backed her."

"I think you mean you backed her."

Drake shrugged.

"I guess I have some credibility with the guys."

Tulla didn't blink. She must be one of the guys.

The drinks cart came around. Agnes had coffee. Drake and Tulla took water. Agnes guessed that Drake drank water on the job, and that Tulla never drank anything else.

The file had been burning into Agnes's lap. It would just get hotter, until she opened it. She surrendered.

Crime scene photos took her back to a road in Puna, the wettest and wildest region of the Big Island. Many Puna roads were mud, but this one was paved.

The first photo was a framing shot of a Ford Escape stopped half on the road and half in the jungle. On this side of the Big Island the rainforest crowded right up to the blacktop, and only constant maintenance kept the roots from tearing up the roads.

The vehicle had challenged an ironwood tree to a collision. The ironwood had won. More photos showed the damage to the front of the Escape and the condition of the tires.

Then things got serious. A woman sat in the front passenger seat. She conformed to the contours of the seat in a boneless kind of way that would have told anyone, not just an experienced observer like Agnes, that she was dead.

Her name was Marci Savage. She was married to Donald Savage, an officer in the Kona Division of the Hawaii County Police. Puna was on the Hilo side of the island, and about as far from Kona as anyone could get.

Most people looked away from the ugliness of violent death, but crime scene photographs focused on it. So did criminal lawyers. Agnes studied three close-ups of the woman's ravaged face.

Agnes became aware that Drake was reading along with her.

"Seatbelts save lives," he said.

"Usually," she said. "But hers held her upright for a second shot."

The next photo showed a man in his forties. He had looked better, but at least he wasn't dead. The only visible damage was a goose egg on his forehead. Drake pointed.

"Is that her husband?"

"Yes. Thanks for the perspective, by the way."

Drake raised his eyebrows.

"I've been obsessing over this case, but most people in the world haven't heard of it."

"He looks like a cop."

"He is. He's also the one who killed her."

"You're sure of that?"

"Look again and tell me what you see."

Drake stared and then nodded. "Self-inflicted injuries to divert suspicion."

"How many times has a killer tried that scam?"

"But they never have the nerve to hurt themselves badly enough. Where is he now?"

"Still on the job. Riding around with a gun, and threatening my client."

"So the case is open."

"Not according to the cops. They say they did their job. The implication is, the prosecutor didn't do his."

"How did your client get in the frame? What's his name, by the way?"

"Hank Alves. He was found wandering around in the rainforest just a few feet away. And a search turned up a rifle leaning against a tree right nearby. A 30.06 that ballistics matched to the bullet in the victim."

"What kind of explanation did he give?"

"Pretty lame. He remembers leaving a restaurant in Hilo. He admits to having a few in the bar. Next thing he knows, he's wandering around in the dark woods with a ferocious headache."

"How did you do it? Get a not guilty, I mean."

"I used the old 'Some other dude did it' defense. The jury bought it."

"Which means they believed you about the husband."

"I had to make them read between the lines. Jurors don't like it when you accuse a cop and don't back it up with hard evidence. But if you make them do the work themselves, they have an investment in the theory."

"Gutsy move."

"It worked. They got what I was telling them, and I believe that's because it's true."

"What was supposed to be your client's motive?"

"That's where I caught a break. They didn't really have much of one. Hank had a nasty encounter with Savage. Basically, a cop throwing his weight around. Make that his fists. But no matter how they dressed it up, it didn't look like enough to kill over. Not unless Hank was complete psychopath, and nobody who sees him can believe that."

"Even so, you must have done a hell of job. There aren't many stories as weak as the self-inflicted wound, but your client found one."

"Tell me about it. To make things worse, he kept insisting about a witness. A hooker he picked up in the bar of the restaurant."

"How did you handle that?"

"I destroyed the bartender on the stand. He denied letting hookers work in his bar, but his record didn't help him. Then I made it sound as if the cops had made the hooker disappear and leaned on the bartender to make him lie. It was all hints, but the jury got it."

"Which made you real popular with the cops."

"I was already high on their hate list."

"If I'm ever looking at serious time, I'll definitely call you."

Drake held his hands out for the file. She passed it to him.

"I suppose you considered the possibility that the husband hired your client?"

"If I tried, maybe I could think of a less likely hitman. But why would I want to?"

4

A CHANGE IN THE SOUND and feel of the engines woke her. Diamond Head showed on the right. Agnes sometimes thought that the real reason for her shopping trips to Los Angeles was the pleasure of coming home. The sight pierced her even through her preoccupation with the case.

They walked to the inter-island terminal rather than do more sitting on the Wiki-Wiki shuttle. The flight to Hilo was brief, but Agnes winced when she saw the seats in the cramped cabin pressing Tulla's knees even harder.

When the seatbelt sign went off overhead, passengers lurched to their feet and started thumbing their cell phones. Agnes usually waited for the futile bustle to subside before getting up, but today she was right there with the most impatient travelers.

Her investigator Lanny answered the second ring.

"I'm back. Everything okay?"

"So far. I hope you brought help. I didn't sign on for this."

"I know. I'll make it up to you."

Nobody could manipulate the internet better or get a witness talking faster than Lanny, but watching for the bad guys and dealing out physical violence didn't appear on his resume.

"I did bring help, and they're as good as it gets."

"Glad to hear it. I have some leads to follow up, and I can't do it like this."

He meant babysitting the client.

"We'll get on the road," she said, and disconnected.

Drake and Tulla stood by with their carry-on bags.

"Let's go," said Agnes.

"Weapons?" said Drake.

"Where we're going."

"I don't like being unarmed."

It couldn't be helped. If the bodyguards had checked any firearms through to Hawaii, the police would find out. But now the guns that Drake had asked for were hours away.

Her Camry waited for them in the long-term lot, which in Hilo was just a few steps away. It was one of the perks of living on an island the size of Connecticut in land area but not much bigger than Bridgeport or New Haven in population.

Agnes took her remote entry fob from her bag and made the car chirp. The sound seemed to provoke the squeal of tires behind her. Even as she flinched, she knew what to expect.

The roaring engine belonged to a black Impala. It had a blue cone mounted on the roof.

"Cops," she said.

Her companions might not know how things worked in Hawaii County. Many police officers used their personal vehicles on duty and got reimbursed for mileage. The blue cone was the only clue to the cops inside.

Drake nodded. Tulla didn't react at all.

Two uniformed officers climbed out of the Impala. Agnes knew them by sight. She had never cross examined them, or she would have remembered their names. Japanese and Portuguese genes showed in both men, and the younger of the two also had enough Hawaiian ancestry to put him over three hundred pounds.

They obviously knew her.

"Don't move," the shorter, older cop told her.

She didn't dignify that with a reply, and she hoped the two bodyguards would take their cue from her.

The big cop made a circular motion with his index finger. Drake and Tulla turned around and raised their arms. The cop began to frisk Drake.

"What is your probable cause?" said Agnes.

"Shut up," said the older cop.

"No. You need an articulable reason to frisk my friends."

"We got a tip that they're carrying."

"Let me guess. Anonymous?"

There was no way to disprove it.

The big cop found Drake's wallet and tossed it to his partner. He went on to Tulla. His hands lingered just a moment too long everywhere he put them. Tulla held very still, and Agnes knew what she was thinking. If the cop pinched her or jabbed her with a pin concealed in his hand, and she reacted, he could then subdue her with all the force he wanted.

Agnes watched closely, but she caught nothing but the too intimate touching.

"No identification," said the big cop. He started to reach for his handcuffs.

Tulla pointed at her own chest and raised her eyebrows

in a question. She took the lack of response from the two cops as permission to fish a travel wallet on a lanyard out of her shirt. The big cop took it from her and handed it to his partner.

"What are you laughing at?" said the big cop.

Tulla said nothing, but she kept smiling. Agnes decided that she never wanted to see that smile directed at her.

For a moment nobody moved. Then the older cop nodded at his partner. Both cops broke away and went to their Impala. When they were settled, the older cop sent the driver's window down.

"Aloha," he said.

The Impala drove off.

"I assume carry permits are with the guns?" said Drake.

"They are," said Agnes. "But now they know you."

"That was going to happen anyway," said Tulla.

There was nothing to do except get going.

"I'll drive," said Agnes. "I know where we're going, and the cops won't try anything so soon after that little scene."

Drake let Tulla have the front passenger seat of the Camry.

"Where are we headed?" asked Drake.

"Keep your eyes open, and then you tell me where you think we are."

Agnes enjoyed showing visitors around her island, and she hadn't had the opportunity for a while. As always, she saw the trip through their eyes. The northbound highway crossed one gulch after another. The three-hour trip would have taken weeks of arduous climbing in the days before the civil engineers had conquered Hawaii. The road made a subtle upgrade until Honoka'a, after which the terrain changed. Grassland began to appear on both sides of the highway, and then the first beef cattle, making inscrutable cow eyes at the passing traffic.

Strip malls and ranching-related businesses started to line the highway. Pickup trucks were well represented in the parking lots, and when the first cowboy in jeans and a flannel shirt emerged from a roadside restaurant, Drake couldn't contain himself.

"How did we get to Wyoming?"

Agnes laughed.

"Just wait. We're going to an actual ranch."

They reached the center of town. Agnes drove through and took the right at the main traffic light. After another five minutes the grade grew even steeper.

"I called in a big favor," she said. "The rancher is the father of another client. The son was charged as a dealer, and I got him simple possession. His father still thinks he owes me."

She glanced in the mirror at Drake.

"Just be prepared. He's a bit of a crackpot. In fact, forget the 'bit' part."

"So why do we need him?"

"He likes to thumb his nose at the government. Including the cops."

"Okay, I guess."

Tulla said nothing. Agnes was starting to wonder what it took to get her to object to something.

Other than being groped by a cop.

Now the car was climbing a serious grade. Agnes passed her favorite scenic overlook, the one that offered a view of the ocean miles away, with nothing in between except space. She would have liked to stop and share it with her guests, but they couldn't afford the exposure. She kept driving upward. The road leveled out at about five thousand feet above sea level. Drake rolled the window down and sampled the crisp high-country air.

"Damn," he said. "This is really disorienting."

"I grew up in Wyoming," said Tulla. "This is sort of close."

She was looking straight ahead, as if the views along the road had nothing to offer her.

"I didn't know that," said Drake in a tone that said anything his partner told them would be more than he knew.

Tulla refused the invitation to elaborate.

Agnes started looking. There was the dirt road she was looking for. She slowed, turned off the pavement, and stopped at a gate that had more than its share of signs on it.

"Kapu."

"Protected by Smith & Wesson."

"What part of 'Keep Out' don't you get?"

"Kapu?" said Drake.

"Forbidden," said Agnes. "It's Hawaiian."

"But no padlocks," said Tulla. "Like he wants somebody to try it."

"Exactly," said Agnes. "I suggested that might be a bad idea for the time being, but he said that doing anything different would be like notifying the cops that he has company. He has a point."

Drake climbed out and opened the gate. He waited for Agnes to drive through and closed up behind her. He got back in the car.

Agnes drove for another mile before the house came into view. Their host was already waiting. Cole Hanbun looked the part of a rancher in his jeans, sheepskin jacket and venerable cowboy hat. The rifle in his hands completed the picture.

Their host's swept-back hair showed white where it overlapped his collar, and the subtropical sun had turned his skin the color of a Gucci suitcase. If he wasn't seventy, he was close.

Agnes parked and got out. A brilliant smile split the

rancher's face.

"My favorite lawyer is back."

"That doesn't take much. I'm the only lawyer you wouldn't shoot on sight."

"Good point. You brought friends."

Agnes made the introductions. Hanbun shook hands with both bodyguards without lingering unduly over his contact with Tulla. No doubt about the capabilities of a woman showed on his face. So far, so good, but Agnes knew her host would soon be testing the forbearance of his guests.

"Welcome. Welcome. There's no such thing as too many friends in the struggle against government tyranny."

There it was, and Agnes knew it would continue. Drake and Tulla handled it well. They made no comment.

"Everything calm here?" she asked.

"So far. I put your man to work."

"That's fair," she said.

In fact, she decided to have a private laugh later. Her client Hank Alves might prefer prison to hard work.

"He's out riding the fences with Thomas."

"How is Thomas?"

"So far, so good."

Agnes reserved judgment on that. She knew how shrewd drug users could be.

"Can we see the arsenal, Cole? My friends feel better when they're equipped."

This was a ticklish moment. She wouldn't put it past Cole to have torn up the carry permits, regarding them as an intolerable infringement of his rights. But he led them to his study. She had been there before, and she knew his gun cabinet. Right there on his desk sat the permits. Drake picked them up and handed one to Tulla. Agnes approved of Drake's silence. He seemed to have picked up on the issue the permits might present.

Cole turned a key in the cabinet. The door swung open to reveal Cole's meticulously maintained arsenal of handguns and rifles. Most of the long guns had beautiful, polished wood stocks, but several had the black steel brutality of modern special forces weaponry.

"I thought you might be a little more state of the art than a dinosaur like me."

"This'll do," said Tulla.

An expression appeared on her face that Agnes could only describe as bliss.

Cole seemed to like Tulla's reaction. He watched as she selected a Glock. Drake took a Smith and Wesson nine-millimeter.

"That's what the local cops use," said Agnes.

"Only fair," said Drake. "I think we should keep a couple of long guns where we can get at them faster."

He gave the host a questioning look.

"We can do that," said Cole.

Agnes heard the front door bang open. Tulla and Drake both came alert. Two male voices came to them. Agnes knew them both. The whiny one was her current client. The petulant tone belonged to Cole's son.

She sometimes daydreamed about having a client she could like.

Both bodyguards shot looks at her, but she nodded her okay.

"Let's go check the damage," said Cole.

One of the things she gave him credit for was his lack of illusions about his son. Family was family, but he also knew that his son didn't measure up. In this situation it helped that Hank didn't make Thomas Hanbun look bad in comparison.

Agnes went back to the living room to greet both men.

Thomas Hanbun saw her first. He snorted with disgust.

"I guess you learn from your mistakes," he said.

Agnes didn't need to ask what he meant. While his father had understood the near miracle she had worked for his son, Thomas thought he should have walked away clean.

"I don't make mistakes," she said, "At least not the kind you could ever catch me at."

"You got him off," said Thomas with a contemptuous wave at Hank.

"It helps when the client didn't do it."

All of this went over Hank's head. He was too busy sniveling over the pain in his lower body. With someone else Agnes would have sympathized. Riding a working horse on a working ranch was hard on the body, and it took years to get used to it, especially for someone as soft as Hank Alves. And Thomas had probably been harder on him than he needed to be.

Tulla and Drake appeared. Agnes made the introductions. Again, Tulla showed nothing, although Agnes would have bet the woman could read the two men as easily as Agnes herself. Drake was smoothly professional, but Agnes could discern the disdain under the surface.

Cole joined them.

"First off," said Agnes, "I don't think it's the best idea to send them out on the ranch. Too exposed."

"You said the cops don't know where they are."

"Sooner or later they will. I laid a false trail, but they won't buy it forever."

"A false trail?"

"Before I went to New Jersey, I borrowed a Jeep and drove Lanny down into Waipi'o. I made sure people saw us. Then I came back up without him."

"Thinking the cops would believe he was Hank, and he's

still hiding out down there?"

"Lanny climbed out after dark. He's still pissed at me."

The idea of a bad guy hiding in the lush Waipi'o Valley would make sense to the police. They usually left the place alone, and the valley's handful of residents pursued their incessant feuds without interference. The residents tended to share Cole's view of the government.

"So we have to sit in the house forever?" said Hank.

"I hope not. I'm working on it. It's a matter of finding evidence against Donald Savage that the cops can't ignore."

"If you're going to go to work," said Drake, "we should too. We need to get out there."

"You'll need horses," said Cole. "You can't cover the ground on foot."

Drake kept his expression close to his usual professional deadpan, but Agnes found that she already knew him well enough to see the panic underneath.

Tulla stepped in.

"I'll ride. Drake will keep static surveillance."

It sounded plausible. Cole looked as if he might even be buying it. Agnes was less pleased. She could see that she needed more operatives on this team. Tulla and Drake couldn't keep up the two-person operation for long, and then they would be working one operative per twelve-hour shift.

Whatever she hoped to accomplish had to happen fast.

She considered waiting for dark before leaving, but she decided that it was more important to be a moving target.

"I'll be using landlines to check in," she told Cole.

Would the cops be surveilling her cell phone electronically? She didn't know, but they were certainly angry enough to break the rules.

Hank followed her out to her car.

"I don't like that guy."

Like everything else he had said lately, the words came out in a whine.

"Cole? He doesn't have to help us, you know."

"No, That Thomas punk. I swear, he was trying to get my neck broken."

"Riding takes some getting used to."

"It was more than that. He kept trying to spook my horse."

"He has a lousy sense of humor. I'll give you that much."

Hank tried to pursue it, but she cut him off.

"If you want to get out of here, let me get to work."

5

AGNES RETRACED THE ROUTE back to Hilo and chafed at the hours it took. Mainlanders often looked at the Hawaiian Islands as specks on the globe, but this island got its nickname for a reason. Residents of the Big Island logged many miles and many hours behind the steering wheel.

Lanny met her at a coffee place in the Prince Kuhio Plaza. To get to him Agnes had to endure a glare from the off-duty cop working mall security.

"Are you all recovered?"

Lanny gave her a glare as good as the cop's.

"No, I'm not recovered. I'm no hiker. That road is some serious shit."

The single road into the Waipi'o Valley was so steep that two-wheel drive vehicles couldn't grip the surface, and hikers almost needed to use their hands to climb out.

"You're always talking about getting into shape. That was

a good start."

"I changed my mind."

Agnes sipped coffee and let him vent.

"Got anything?" she asked him.

"Nothing much," he said in a tone that told her he had something very good. "How about an internal affairs file on Don Savage?"

"Interesting. Recent?"

"Since the trial."

"What's the issue?"

"Shaking down hookers."

"How did you find out?"

"Hawaii County Police. Four hundred brothers in blue, right?"

"I guess you're going to tell me something different."

"Savage has some colleagues who are less than fans."

"Can we keep this to ourselves for now?"

"I was careful about meeting my informant, and he definitely was too. But who knows?"

"Who are the hookers?"

"My informant had one name. Tiffany Cobb. I got an address in Keauhou."

"Makes sense."

That was condo territory, just south of Kona on the dry side of the island. The town was full of retirees and other affluent transplants from the mainland. Many people came for a few weeks or months and then moved on without anyone thinking twice about it.

Of course, it meant another three or four hours in the car, this time around the southern tip of the island, with many reduced speed limits through one small town after another. On the plus side were some of the most stunning ocean views in Hawaii. Agnes was a lifelong resident, but she never tired of them.

As always in Keauhou, parking was tight. The address they were looking for proved to be a two-story, eight-unit condo. Agnes and Lanny climbed an open-air staircase to the second floor.

Lanny pressed the doorbell. They listened to the buzz inside. It was the only sound. He rang again.

"Shit," said Agnes.

It was quite a trip for nothing. But then Lanny tried the door handle. It turned. He raised his eyebrows at Agnes, who looked around. There might be a busybody behind one of the many nearby windows, but the midday silence reassured her. In a neighborhood full of vacationers, few people wasted daylight hours in rented quarters.

"Let's do it," she said.

It was a risk, but this woman was supposedly a prostitute. If she came home and found uninvited company, she might try to get tough, but she wouldn't bring the cops in.

Lanny entered first, with Agnes close behind. She found herself in a living room decorated in high-concept Hawaiian tacky. In the center of the room was a coffee table in imitation koa wood. Mail and magazines covered it. Agnes picked up a stack of bills and junk mail. Everything that wasn't addressed to "Our Neighbor At" was to Tiffany Cobb.

"Two bedrooms," said Lanny.

"Let's get started."

Lanny went to the bathroom. Agnes started with the first bedroom, which was neat enough to make her feel inadequate. That was a problem. Her own bedroom would tell a snoop a lot about her, but this woman's neatness hid more than it revealed.

The other bedroom looked like the guest room of a woman who hadn't had a guest in a while, and who had nothing to store. The closet was empty.

Too empty. Agnes began to feel the presence of a ghost. She went and found Lanny, who had moved to the kitchen.

"I'm getting the idea that somebody else lived here until very recently."

"I know what you mean," he said. "Nothing I can put my finger on."

The plastic trash receptacle had a white bag neatly turned down over its rim. Lanny gathered the mouth of the bag and lifted it out. He knew his job, and searching the garbage was a big part of it.

But first he glanced inside the garbage can.

"Hello."

6

HE REACHED INSIDE and picked for a moment at something. His hand emerged holding a scrap of paper. Agnes went to him for a look

It was a mailing label, or rather, half of a label, torn vertically. Its adhesive backing had stuck it to the inside of the canister.

"Katie O …," Agnes read. "13110 A … Keouhou …"

13110 Akipuna Street was this address.

"Like Katie O sanitized the place, but missed this?"

"Which makes us want to know why she up and left," said Lanny.

The rest of the garbage told them nothing new.

"That was interesting," said Agnes on the sidewalk in front of the building. "It's time to check in with Cole."

"On a land line," said Lanny.

They gave each other blank looks. This was like going

back to the Nineteen Eighties. No, it was even harder, because back then pay phones had been everywhere. Now they were almost extinct.

"Come on," she said. "You're supposed to be a detective."

"Not a magician. Maybe the hotels still have pay phones."

They drove south on Ali'i Drive. The first big hotel was the Royal Kona resort.

"Damn," said Lanny. "I wasn't thinking. I know a guy works there. At least, I think he still does."

They went around back to the pool and open-air bar. Lanny and the bartender exchanged grins and handshakes, after which the man set a twentieth-century touch tone phone on the bar. He went down to the other end of the bar and started polishing glasses.

Good bartenders always knew how to pick up on the nuances.

"I think I remember how to do this," said Agnes.

Cole Hanbun picked up on the third ring.

"I was about to take a chance on your cell," he said.

"Why? What happened?"

"Somebody took a shot at your boy."

"Where, in the house? Is everybody okay?"

"They were out working. Nobody got hurt."

Agnes bit down on a cutting remark before it could escape. Cole didn't have to help her at all, and Hank was probably getting on his nerves. Getting him out of the house had probably saved him from death at Cole's hands.

"I have to go up to Kohala," she told Lanny.

"What do you want me to do? Katie O?"

"Or Tiffany Cobb. Whichever you find first."

7

THAT LED TO MORE DRIVING, this time through the desert. Agnes schooled herself to patience, as the familiar landmarks ticked by in their own time—the turnoff for the Saddle Road, the cactus plants on the approach to Waimea, and then the relentless climb to 5,000 feet. Her Camry complained, but there was nothing to be done about that.

Tulla came on horseback to meet the car. Agnes stopped and sent her window down.

"What do we know?"

"Not much. I was with the principal. Drake was riding the perimeter."

"Drake is riding now?"

"He had to learn, so he did."

"So what happened?"

"Thomas had Hank fixing a fence. Thomas went off to do something. Next thing I know, Hank drops the post he's working with, and right on top of that I hear a shot. I threw him down and covered him."

Agnes spared a hundredth of a second on imagining Tulla on top of her.

"So the sound was delayed."

"Right. Pretty long shot."

"Did you get a trajectory?"

"Just a guess, but if I'm right, the son should have seen something. Assuming he was where he says he was."

Tulla wasn't about to tell Agnes how to do her job, but Agnes already knew she had to question Thomas Hanbun.

"What about the paniolo?"

It wasn't Tulla's style to look puzzled, or ask for help.

"Sorry," said Agnes. "The cowboys."

Cole employed about a half-dozen hands.

"Guess we'll have to ask them."

Twilight didn't last long in the subtropical latitudes. The cowboys had gathered in the bunkhouse-cookhouse building behind Cole's residence. Agnes considered the options and turned to Tulla.

"You up for questioning them?"

"Sure."

The hands had seen Tulla riding as if she had been born on horseback. That had probably earned her some respect. So did her familiarity with firearms and the I-can-take-you vibe she broadcast.

The six paniolo sitting around their mess table or reclining on bunks were wiry, mostly Portuguese men, and if they were true to the type, they were fourth or fifth generation cowboys. Tulla pulled a stool up to the end of the table and sat.

"You all heard about what happened?"

Nods all around. They were twenty-first century ranch

hands, who rode with two-way radios. Cell phone coverage up here was improving but still iffy.

But in the end Tulla couldn't do much beyond going around the room and getting shrugs and head shakes. Nobody had seen anything.

"Let me go relieve Drake," Tulla said finally.

Drake walked as if he had been kicked simultaneously in the balls and the ass.

"If you laugh, I quit."

"I wouldn't dream of it."

Agnes snorted and then laughed out loud.

"I'm sorry. I'm sure I'd look even worse."

"You have to resolve this situation," he said. "And not just to save my tender ass."

"What do you mean?"

"The cops are staking the place out."

She hadn't expected the hideout to last forever, but this was still bad news. Agnes made a decision.

"I'll go talk to them."

"I'm coming," said Cole.

"Cole, is that a good idea?"

"My property."

In other words, not open to negotiation. And now Agnes couldn't even change her mind about confronting the police, because Cole would go without her and make a bad situation worse.

She drove to the front gate. Cole followed on horseback. He liked to talk down to the minions of the government.

Agnes wouldn't have been surprised to see the two cops from the airport, but these two took her by surprise.

"Counselor," said Detective Coutinho.

Officer Jenny Freitas was with him. Agnes knew the young woman as one of the good ones. It stood to reason, if

Coutinho had her tag along.

"Has the news gotten around?" she said.

"That you're with Hanbun?"

At that moment Cole rode up.

"Can you read, Cop?"

"That's Detective. We're not on your property."

"Well, somebody was. Somebody took a shot at my guest. I don't care who you are, I shoot back."

Agnes cursed silently. Now she couldn't find out whether Coutinho had already known about the attack.

But he gave her one for free, and she realized that he knew what he was doing. Coutinho always did.

"We overheard some radio traffic, and we know where it happened. That's a crime scene, and we need to investigate."

"Do you have a warrant?"

Cole was just throwing up roadblocks, Agnes knew. A warrant wouldn't make him any more cooperative. It came from the government that he refused to recognize.

"We don't need a warrant," Coutinho said. "We have permission from the Bishop estate."

"That's my land."

"You want us to think so. We always told you that treating Bishop land as your own would come back to bite you someday. Today is the day."

The Bishop estate owned much of the island, but a century of bad record keeping had made it impossible to know which parcels of land were which.

"When you bring that warrant, bring an army, too."

Cole jerked the reigns and rode back toward the house. He didn't just want the last word. Agnes knew he was going to rally his troops. She wondered whether his cowboys would really back him after all these years of trash talk about jackbooted government thugs.

Who were coming because he was repaying a debt to her that he didn't owe in the first place.

She watched Coutinho walk back to his own Wrangler. He was going to summon the Special Response Team, the large men in black who broke down doors and deployed serious firepower. She could think of nothing to do except get back in the car.

8

AT THE HOUSE she saw that Cole was rousing his troops. He had his paniolo gathered in the living room, where Agnes knew they usually weren't allowed. They all stood, too ill at ease to sit.

Thomas and Hank didn't have that issue. They lounged on opposite ends of a leather sofa.

"This is it," Cole bellowed. "This is the day I always knew would come. Are you with me?"

Six weather-beaten faces looked back at him. Cole went on as if they had all bellowed back.

"Arm yourselves. We have the fight of our lives coming."

He turned and saw Agnes.

"Where are your people? We need them."

"They're out keeping watch."

"Get them."

"Cole, their job is to guard the principal, not to fight the police."

"The principal is with me. Right, Hank?"

Again, Cole didn't wait for a reply. If he had really looked, Hank's slack-jawed stare would not have reassured him.

"Let's go," said Cole.

The six cowboys shuffled out of the room, with Cole behind them, urging them forward. Thomas Hanbun followed without enthusiasm.

"Hank," said Agnes.

"Yeah?"

"Who shot at you?"

"How would I know?"

"Could it have been Thomas?"

"Well, he wasn't right there with me. But I don't think he hates me that much. Only the cops do."

She studied him, but all she saw was the same general untrustworthiness he always broadcast.

"Let's go see if we can stop anybody from getting killed."

Hank didn't move.

"Come on, Hank. This is all about you in the first place."

Immediately she wondered how to follow through on her big talk. She didn't know where they were going, and they certainly weren't going to get there in her two-wheel drive sedan. But outside one of the cowboys waited with four horses, saddled and ready. One was for him, and the others, she realized, were for her, Thomas, and Hank.

The paniolo was not much of a talker. He helped her up onto her horse and then mounted his own. He slapped her horse to get it moving and led the way uphill.

It would have made a very pleasant outing. The air was crisp at this altitude, and the alpine scenery world-class. But Agnes couldn't think about anything but the mayhem that awaited her.

After about fifteen minutes Agnes felt herself adjusting

to the sway of the horse, and she found that the animal took the suggestions she made with the reins. Her cowboy escort must have chosen this mount with her in mind.

The paniolo was in no hurry. Agnes found herself surging ahead of the party.

The crest of the slope was in sight about a hundred yards away, when she heard the shot. Agnes cringed, but nothing followed.

"Who was that?" she asked the cowboy.

"Thirty-ought-six."

It was a tactful way of saying that Cole had taken the shot with one of his near-antiques. How bad was it going to be when she got there?

Agnes reached the highest point and looked downhill. Cole Hanbun lay prone with a large knee belonging to a large man planted in the middle of his back. The tactical officer was cuffing Cole's hands behind him. Cole's cheek pressed into the vivid green of the grass.

What shocked her was the pity that overwhelmed her. She didn't share Cole's views, but here was his worst nightmare come true. Inches from his nose, filling his field of vision, was a size thirteen jackboot.

Her instincts took over. She started looking around for facts on the ground. Who were her witnesses? Who was bleeding?

Coutinho was there, and Jenny Freitas. In addition to the SRT officer dealing with Cole, two other men in black stood by. Cole's cowboys seemed to have disappeared.

Agnes approached Coutinho.

"Anybody hurt?"

"No. One shot, wild."

He reached into the pocket of his police windbreaker.

"We have a warrant."

With another cop she would have read every word, but she waved the paper away. Coutinho didn't cheat.

"I assume Cole is under arrest."

"It depends."

"On what?"

"His cooperation. I'm thinking it might have been an accidental discharge of a legal firearm."

"Let me talk to my client."

Coutinho nodded at the SRT with Cole. The officer stood and backed away. That left Agnes to help Cole up. A seventy-year-old man in handcuffs wasn't going to manage it on his own. Agnes could have wept at the humiliation and impotence on her client's face.

"The police have their job to do," she said. "Now might be the time for a little compromise."

"Compromise with oppression, and you've lost the war."

"Maybe it's time to let someone else do the fighting for a while."

"Who, Thomas?"

There it was, the contempt that Cole had carefully contained all through his son's drug problems and skirmishes with the legal system.

"Stand back and let him step up. He might surprise you."

Agnes doubted it, and in fact she hoped not. Cole's obsessions deserved to go extinct. But that would come another time. This was now, and it wasn't the first time she had said what she needed to say to achieve a result.

And then tried to live with herself.

Agnes looked around and saw a tree stump that looked flat and level enough for sitting. She guided Cole the dozen steps to it, watching his footing carefully.

She was going deeper and deeper into a situation that she didn't welcome.

Agnes looked at Coutinho, who gave her a slight nod. He beckoned Hank and Thomas to him.

"Mr. Alves, where were you when the shots came?"

Hank pointed downhill toward a stream that slashed across a treeless expanse of grass and rock outcrops.

"Thomas told me to clear some brush out of the stream. It was catching stuff and interfering with the flow."

"Mr. Hanbun, where were you?"

Thomas pointed east, parallel to the summit of the ridge.

"Riding the fences. You can't see them from here."

Coutinho walked Hank away from Thomas. Agnes followed, expecting the detective to order her away. To her surprise, he didn't.

"Then what, Mr. Alves?"

"I had a hold of this branch. I'm pulling on it, and something hits the wood, like two inches from my grip. Knocks the whole thing out of my hands. Stung like a bitch, and I'm thinking, what the hell? Then I hear this sound, like a crack. And then I'm thinking, shit. Somebody just shot at me."

"Stay here, please."

Coutinho started back toward Thomas. Agnes fell into step beside him.

"I can think of about three hundred suspects," she said. "Or maybe just one."

"I hope you don't mean us."

"Did I say the Hawaii County Police?"

"You didn't say Don Savage, either. But it's pretty clear who you meant."

Coutinho stopped and looked around.

"What a nightmare."

Agnes knew he meant the crime scene, which took in a couple of square miles. That was the problem with a rifle.

"Where are your people?"

"Around," said Agnes. "Doing their job."

"I need to talk to them."

"I'll get them back to the house. One at a time."

Coutinho didn't argue the point. He turned to Officer Freitas.

"Uncuff him."

Freitas didn't blink. Agnes had to admire their teamwork. She approached Cole, and as the handcuffs fell away, she took over with a hand on his wrist.

"Not a word," she said. "Let's go home."

He obeyed like an elderly father with his favorite daughter. Agnes felt her throat closing again, and she felt relieved when he required no further words from her.

It might have something to do with her own father, who was as near as Google, and as far as anyone could be.

When she reached her horse, she unhooked her handheld radio from the saddle. First Drake and then Tulla answered.

"I need one of you at the house."

Her voice worked. That was good.

"Correction. The cops need you. One or the other to start."

"On my way," said Drake, sounding as laconic as a cowboy.

Agnes suppressed an unhelpful urge to giggle at Drake's transformation.

9

COUTINHO LET HANK GO after only an hour or so. He was cutting her some slack, although he would deny it if she ever forgot herself so far as to thank him. She stowed Hank in her car and started toward the highway.

Agnes was relieved to reach Waimea without burning her brakes out, but that was only one of her worries, and not the most intractable. Now she had to think of another place to stash Hank Alves. She believed the pressure was off at least a bit, now that there was a record of an attempt to kill him, but desperation could make even a cop panic.

One thing occurred to her, and she was already in the neighborhood, by Big Island standards. She turned west, toward the driest part of the island. The Kohala resorts squatted there among scrub brush and flat black volcanic rock. The landscape looked unpromising, but it had two precious things. Behind the stark terrain lurked the island's best beaches, and

43

sunshine was as close to a certainty as anything in this life.

The desk clerk covered his surprise well. She was a week-end regular, but he had never seen her on Wednesday before. Agnes didn't see a signal, but the day manager appeared a moment later.

"I need a room, Enrique, and can you accommodate my friend?"

"For you, Ms. Rodrigues, we always have something."

Enrique prospered by anticipating the needs of his guests. She didn't even have to mention her preference for a budget room, or as close to budget at it got in this hotel. He also understood that she had things on her mind other than her usual weekend routine of picking up a married man from the mainland in the hotel bar.

She registered Hank under his own name. The cops would find him anyway, and if they wanted to make a run at him here, they would at least have to put a veneer of legitimacy on it.

"You should be okay," she told Hank. "But it would still be a good idea to stay in the room as much as possible."

She expected him to whine, and he delivered. She gave him a minute and then cut him off.

"Hank, if somebody took a shot at me, I would sure as hell learn something from the experience."

That shut him up, which allowed her to hear Lanny's ring tone sounding in her bag.

"Guess who flew to the mainland earlier today."

Agnes said nothing. Right now Lanny's usual teasing game wasn't going to play, and her silence made him realize it. He went on quickly.

"I'll give you a hint. We were guests in her home recently."

"Tiffany Cobb," she said. "Perfect."

Agnes blew air out. It would be helpful if she could

arrange a welcome party in Los Angeles or Vegas or wherever. The cops could do that, but they weren't about to help her with these two witnesses.

"Anybody named Katie with her?"

"No hint that she's traveling with anyone."

"That leaves nobody to talk to but Don Savage. Good thing I have an idea about that."

It wasn't until the next morning that she was able to sit with Drake and Tulla over breakfast at the hotel. Both operatives were tired and showing it. They had experience in working through their exhaustion, but Agnes still needed to make something happen soon.

"I got a read on Savage during Hank's trial," she said. "I think he's a user when it comes to women."

"Hookers are easy to use," said Drake. "Just pay them."

"But controlling them takes technique."

"Good point."

"I'll bet your boss let the clients think they were using her, while she stayed in control."

"I also think they don't make many like her."

"We're going to need her."

"I doubt she'll come out here. She really doesn't want to see Hawaii again."

"She won't have to."

Agnes turned to Tulla.

"I need you to stretch yourself a little. Maybe a lot."

10

TULLA WAS ALREADY SHAKING her head. She knew what was coming. That was good and bad. Good, because it meant the woman had the smarts that the situation required. Bad, because she didn't like it and would push back hard.

"If there was another way," said Agnes, "we'd take it."

"I don't do that shit."

"You won't have to do anything but get him talking."

"I know what that means. Pillow talk."

Tulla's glare ranked up there with a multiple murderer Agnes had defended.

"Maybe not. Let's call your boss."

"For pointers?"

That was part of what Agnes wanted. A direct order from Tulla's boss would also help, but if it came to that, Agnes wanted to give Tulla some privacy. Agnes signed the breakfast check and went out to the lobby to see Enrique.

"I need a meeting room."

"Of course, Ms. Rodrigues."

It was a new request from her, but he betrayed no surprise. Agnes knew this resort got its share of Type A personalities who never stopped working. Enrique sent her down a corridor she had never used before. The room was marked with a number only. People who came to get away from work didn't want to see anyone else doing it.

Agnes made the call and put her cell phone on speaker. It was noon in New Jersey, but if Diana Andrews was at lunch, she gave no hint.

"I have a job for Tulla," said Agnes. "I need her to get close to Don Savage."

Andrews skipped several links in the chain of thought.

"You're thinking he likes a challenge."

Six feet of forbidding beauty certainly qualified.

"That's my impression."

"Tulla, you up for this?" said Andrews.

What was Tulla going to say to a woman who wasn't just her boss, but could also have handled the assignment herself without breaking a sweat?

"I can't do the girlie girl thing. Not so anybody would believe it."

"We don't want you to," said Andrews. "We want you to be yourself. It'll be a change of pace from what he's used to. I used to do that all the time with clients, especially the veterans. Corporate one time, biker chick the next."

"I also can't do the pickup thing. No experience."

If Tulla had been the squirming type, she would have been falling out of her chair.

"Let him come to you. Be reserved. You can take him or leave him."

"That part is true."

"Use it. And here's something that took me a while to learn in my old business. Ninety percent of the job was listening. Sex was ten percent."

"Try zero percent."

Agnes tried to send a telepathic message—don't argue the point.

But Andrews was way ahead of her.

"In the beginning I was surprised how many guys have to pay a woman to listen to them. You're in control."

Everyone sat around the table, looking at the cell phone in the middle as if it were a ouija board.

"Where are you going to find this guy?" Andrews asked finally.

"That part I know," said Agnes. "It came out in the trial. Don Savage hangs out at the brew pub."

"Kona," said Andrews. "I know it. Have an IPA for me."

11

AGNES CALLED LANNY and told him what she needed. Around noon he arrived. He supervised wiring Tulla up.

Kona was a straight shot thirty miles down 19, but Agnes knew enough to leave time. They left at two in the afternoon. As always, traffic stopped miles above Kona and inched the rest of the way. Agnes kept watching Tulla in the mirror. Today the pace of traffic was agonizing rather than just annoying, and Agnes could see it working on the woman's nerves.

"Almost there."

Agnes turned right into the industrial park.

Just after four in the afternoon the parking lot was half full. At night cars would line the streets of the entire industrial area. Agnes pointed at a Ford Bronco with license plates that were burned into her brain, like everything else about Don Savage.

"He's here."

"You really think he's not going to know I'm wired?"

"He's overconfident. We haven't laid a glove on him yet."

Tulla looked unconvinced.

"Even if he does," said Agnes, "he'll just get up and go. Nothing to worry about."

The bodyguard sat still for a moment.

"Let's get it over with."

Tulla opened the rear door with such force that it would have caused a couple thousand dollars' worth of damage to a nearby vehicle. Fortunately, the adjacent parking space was empty. She half ran to the entrance to the pub. Agnes hoped she would get herself under control, or the bartender would see her coming and call 911.

"What if he's just not into her?" Drake asked.

"He will be, or I don't know men."

12

LANNY'S EQUIPMENT WAS top of the line. It picked up and separated the various conversations in the pub with such clarity that Agnes could have blackmailed any number of cheating spouses.

But for three long minutes nothing useful came through.

"What'll you have?" said a new male voice, close to the microphone.

"Pilsner," said Tulla.

"Get that for you?" said another male voice.

The fidelity of the sound thrust Agnes back into the courtroom, facing Dan Savage with nothing but a polished wood railing between them. The smirk never left his face. It was always difficult to rattle a veteran cop with many hours of experience in testifying. She knew she had won because of the not guilty verdict, but she still didn't feel like a winner.

"Thanks," said Tulla with just the right amount of reserved

cordiality.

Agnes knew the tone well. She used it most Saturday nights. She could see the dance as it progressed. Tulla would nod at the stool next to hers, and he would slide onto it.

"I'm Don."

"Tulla. You married, Don?"

Agnes winced. That was a little abrupt. She specialized in married men, and she had learned to ease into the question of status while making it clear that it wasn't a deal breaker.

"No. You?"

"I'm not. You're divorced?"

"What makes you say that?"

"Just betting the odds."

"I'm a widower."

"I'm sorry. You're young for that. I guess your wife was too."

Ouch, Agnes thought.

The only good thing about Tulla's clumsiness was its authenticity, which came though even without visual clues.

"Do you do this much?" said Savage.

His tone said that he had chosen his tactic for this encounter—to meet bluntness with bluntness.

"No," said Tulla. "I usually drink IPA."

That brought a chuckle from Savage, and also from Agnes and Drake. It was a good thing this audio surveillance went only one way.

Drake typed a note into his iPhone and showed Agnes.

"B+?"

Agnes smiled and nodded as she kept listening. From her it would have been a C performance, but Tulla was learning fast.

"Matter of fact, my wife was murdered."

This was progressing so fast that Agnes felt like feeling

with her foot for a brake pedal. She had expected an hour of verbal fencing before this revelation.

"My God."

There was silence, as Tulla groped for something to say. Agnes would have been hard pressed herself.

"I've seen that look before. You're doing the arithmetic."

"Caught me."

"Usually, when a married woman is murdered, it's her husband who did it. But here I am telling you about it."

"That occurred to me."

"So the next question, is did somebody else do it, or did I get away with it?"

"Well?"

"The outcome was the second worst possible. From my point of view, anyway. I wasn't charged, but the guy who was, got acquitted."

"Did he do it?"

"I don't know."

"Seriously?"

"In the beginning I was convinced he did, but the stuff that came out at trial ... I just don't know."

"Are the cops still investigating?"

"I am the cops."

"Oh."

"I wasn't involved in the investigation. I couldn't be, for any number of reasons. But from the standpoint of the department it's over. And that's bad for me."

"No closure."

Agnes blinked. She usually disliked that word, but it was the right thing to say. Tulla was surpassing expectations.

"Not just that. Some cops think I did it."

Agnes told herself to close her mouth. This was completely new to her. Coutinho hadn't given her a hint, but he wouldn't. It would help to know who was who in this power struggle. It might explain who had taken the first shot at Hank, and the second, but cops on both sides of the question would stonewall her.

It occurred to her that a place to start might be the two cops who had harassed her team at the airport.

"I gotta get back to the office for a bit. You want to have dinner tonight?"

That was Savage confounding her again. He didn't match the alpha male she had seen in the courthouse.

"I would like that," said Tulla.

"Huggo's is fun. Seven o'clock?"

"You're on."

13

IT CERTAINLY LOOKED LIKE Don Savage who left the pub and climbed into the Bronco parked near the door. And the woman who followed five minutes later certainly resembled Tulla, but one look at the woman's face told Agnes to save the reprimand for another time. Tulla didn't look in the mood for criticism.

She climbed into the back seat and challenged everyone with a look.

"I didn't get anything," she said.

"We were listening. You did great."

"But you weren't looking at him. I was. I didn't get anything, because there's nothing to get. He didn't kill her."

Agnes opened her mouth to contradict the words, but nothing came out. In an instant she understood the problem. Hank Alves was innocent. That was already messing with her ability to argue whatever point she needed to argue.

She didn't need a new complication, but here it was.

She no longer believed that Don Savage had killed his wife.

"Tulla," she said, "you can't keep this date tonight."

"Then I quit."

Agnes looked at the other woman and saw the problem. Tulla was in love, and for the first time in her life. It was a long time since Agnes had seen that expression on her own face in the mirror, but she remembered it.

"Then we all need to go."

She met Tulla's eyes with her own and hoped the message was clear. This was not negotiable.

14

DON SAVAGE'S EYES FASTENED on Agnes the moment she entered Huggo's. Once again she had to dismiss her immediate attraction to the alpha male. She remembered cross-examining him during Hank's trial and wondering whether they would tear each other's clothes off and fuck their brains out right there on the defense table.

But this time the voltage was lacking in the look he gave her. It came back when he turned to Tulla.

"Do you really need a lawyer?"

"Don," said Tulla, "we need to talk."

Agnes glanced at Tulla, who must be the only woman on the planet who didn't know how those four words affected the male of the species.

First love at thirty instead of thirteen could be awkward.

The hostess was good. She came forward and guided the party to a larger table, deeper inside the restaurant. They wouldn't have their romantic ocean view, but romance was already ruined for the evening.

With everyone seated, Agnes toyed with her water glass and wondered how to begin.

With a frontal assault, of course.

"Don, I thought you killed Marci. I don't think so anymore."

"What changed your mind?"

"You did."

He turned to Tulla.

"You were wired."

Tulla met his eyes and didn't flush. Agnes was impressed.

"That was my job. It's not anymore. I quit."

"Let's wait on that," said Agnes. "Maybe you can help Don more by working with us."

She watched Tulla considering the idea.

"Okay."

"We need to prove who did."

"My colleagues think your client did," said Savage.

"No. Trust me on this. I know you didn't, and I know he didn't."

"Okay, leave that for now. What can we do just sitting here?"

"Throw out ideas."

Now no one seemed to have any.

"Okay," said Agnes. "Who could have taken those shots at Hank Alves? Two different occasions, now."

"I only know about the first one," said Savage. "Internal Affairs couldn't put anyone on the scene."

He challenged Agnes with a look, and she understood. He had someone feeding him details from the internal investigation.

"This second time, I don't know, but I can't see anybody

being that stupid."

"Speaking of stupid, we had a cop hassle the other day."

Agnes gave Savage a description.

"Baclan and Perez."

"They're on your side within the department?"

"Yeah. I didn't tell them to do that, though. I would have told them not to."

"Will they meet with us if you tell them to?"

"After that, they'd better."

"Where is Coutinho on this?"

"Coutinho is all about the evidence. Practically everybody thinks he's a pain in the ass."

"Freitas doesn't. Is she sleeping with him?"

Savage gave Agnes a look that asked, "Why do you care?" She deserved it for blurting.

He got up and plucked his cell phone off the tabletop. Savage let his other hand brush Tulla's shoulder as he went past her toward the restroom. Tulla's eyes closed, and a smile made her lips twitch before she caught herself and smoothed her expression. Agnes looked away, embarrassed for someone.

Herself, probably.

Savage came back.

"Baclan and Perez will meet you tomorrow at Tex. Ten AM, give or take. They'll be on shift, which means they might be late if something is going on. I told them to play nice."

"We'll talk again," said Agnes.

"I know."

15

SHE, LANNY AND DRAKE got up. Tulla didn't move, and her expression said she didn't plan to. Agnes knew she couldn't win this one.

"I'll need you in Honoka'a tomorrow," she said.

Tulla nodded, and Agnes hoped the woman had heard.

Now Agnes faced another Big Island drive. She thought for a moment and called a former client in the small town of Honoka'a. He agreed to house guests for the night.

Just before ten the next morning they took an outdoor table at Tex, right off the highway in Honoka'a. The restaurant was a hazard of the kind that Agnes tried to avoid. Tex made the best malasadas on the island, and she could seldom afford the calories. Nor could she resist them if they were right at hand. A weakness for Portuguese-style donuts was genetic.

Lanny understood. He went to the counter for coffee and

a sugared donut for each of them.

"One and done," he told her. "I'm watching you."

The two cops were only fifteen minutes late. Savage had some serious clout with them. That didn't mean they were feeling cordial. Lanny got up and went to the counter again. If he offered the cops anything, they would have to refuse, but it would be different if the donuts just appeared.

"Thanks for coming," said Agnes.

"Wasn't our idea," said Baclan, the older, smaller cop.

"You're here to help Don Savage. Hank Alves can't be charged with killing Marci Savage, but her husband could be."

"He didn't kill her."

"I agree."

That got their attention.

"You help me figure out who did kill her, and the cloud he's undergoes away. I think that's what you want."

"Yeah," said Perez, the bruiser.

His partner was still reserving judgment.

"I think it might come back to this hooker habit of Don's. Tiffany Cobb. Know the name?"

Two more microscopic nods.

"Okay, somebody named Katie?"

Now the two cops gave her identical blank looks. Agnes began to get an idea of the problem.

"I don't care," she said. "You had some kind of deal with Tiffany, that's up to you. But if I'm going to help Don Savage, I need to know."

"We had an arrangement. Some guys in Hilo Division and some in Kona."

"What kind of arrangement? A don't-shit-where-you-eat kind of thing?"

Baclan flinched a little at the vulgarity from a woman.

Good. It gave her the initiative.

"Tell me if I have this down. You guys in Hilo Division went to Kona to get laid for free. If anybody saw you on that side of the island, they'd be less likely to know you."

Many Big Island residents lived as if Hilo and Kona were on different planets.

"And Kona Division cops came over here for the same reason."

"Yeah," said Perez. "Some of them."

"Okay. Who handled the Hilo side of the transaction?"

"Rachel Park."

"Oh."

Agnes had represented Rachel several times. Her professional name was Tiffany.

Add Tiffany Cobb, and that was too much coincidence. What did it mean?

She was reluctant to let the cops go, now that she had them here and cooperating, but she couldn't think of anything else to ask.

"Thanks for your time, Officers."

They said nothing as they got up and went to their Impala.

16

"LANNY," SAID AGNES, "I know you've been through it, but we're desperate."

He nodded. "Dig deeper on Tiffany Cobb. See if I can find Katie O."

"We'll go talk to Rachel. And we'll find out what the hell happened to Tulla."

Lanny smirked.

"If that's what it is, her boss might have to hear about it."

Lanny removed the smirk. He knew when she was serious.

She took Drake with her and drove south on 19. At Ken's House of Pancakes, she kept going straight on Kalanianaole. As they reached the first of the local beaches on the left, Agnes said, "You have a new experience coming."

Drake didn't reply.

"This?" he asked as they left the paved highway and continued on dirt.

"This."

They had entered the Third World. Shacks and disabled vehicles lined both sides of the road. Large men and women almost as formidable gave the Camry sideways looks as it cruised slowly enough to deal with the craters in the hardened mud road. No one looked friendly. Drake schooled his expression, but it didn't take much to follow his train of thought. No one here worried him physically, but a bodyguard avoided fights that were irrelevant to business.

"You're with me," she said. "I'm not exactly popular, but everybody knows they might need me."

"Professionally, I take it."

"Court-appointed counsel. I get a lot of those."

"What's Rachel Park like?"

"Like Hawaii. The name is Korean, but she looks like me. Mostly Portuguese, in other words. The ethnic melting pot in action."

There was the place Agnes remembered from her last visit a year ago. Rachel had gone an unusually long time between legal problems. Agnes turned right onto packed dirt. The recent drought could be a good thing in situations like this. Rachel's front yard was often treacherous mud.

Agnes and Drake climbed out of her Camry. She led the way to the front door, which looked new, as if someone had liberated it from a construction site. Agnes knocked and then knocked again. She turned the knob, and the door opened.

"Should we?" Drake asked.

"I've been here so many times, I'm almost family."

She pushed the door open. The shack was just one room, with a cot in the far right corner. A free-standing wardrobe next to the cot formed a sleeping nook. It stood open, revealing a collection of pricey corporate-looking garments. On the top shelf were two wig stands. One had a red wig draped over it, but the other was vacant.

"Rachel cleans up well," said Agnes. "She probably charges more than Diana Andrews did in her day. Of course, Diana would get a higher rate here, too. Everything is more expensive."

Drake looked around.

"She's not spending it here."

"She has kids staying with her mother. She supports them all."

Agnes considered writing her a note but decided against it. It might fall into the wrong hands.

As they left the structure, they saw that a teenage boy had taken a seat in a folding beach chair in front of the neighboring shack. He was already well over two hundred pounds, and probably hard at work on a case of diabetes.

"Howzit," said Agnes.

"Miss Rodrigues," said the boy. "You looking for Rachel?"

"Yes."

"She left a little while ago. With some guy."

"A moke?"

"No, just a haole."

Not a local multi-ethnic tough guy, but a white man. It wouldn't be business. Rachel didn't bring clients home.

"A cop?"

Now he looked at her with disappointment, as if she had insulted him.

"Don't I know one cop?"

"Sorry. So, a guy. Kama'aina?"

Meaning, did he look like a long-time resident?

"Long time out in the sun."

"Did it look like she wanted to go with him?"

"They didn't have no kine beef I could see."

Agnes thought about white guys on her island. She turned to Drake.

"Let's go back inside. My reflexes are off. We should have Lanny here."

Lanny never skipped going through the trash. It was often the most revealing thing about a subject.

17

BUT BACK INSIDE the shack she understood why she hadn't thought of the trash. There wasn't any. The place was shabby but clean. Drake caught her train of thought.

"Smell that?" he asked.

"What?"

"Something's been burned. Not too long ago."

"I think you're right."

"Let's check out back," he said.

Behind the shack, set far enough away for fire safety, they found a fifty-gallon steel drum. The smell of a recent fire grew stronger as they approached. Agnes peered over the edge at the bottom of the drum.

"Can you reach that stuff?"

"No," said Drake. "I'll have to dump it. I'll try to keep it together."

He deposited a dozen or so sheets of standard typing or

ALBERT TUCHER

printing paper that the flames hadn't consumed completely. Agnes stooped and picked up the top sheet. On it someone had signed the same name repeatedly.

"Tiffany. Tiffany. Tiffany …"

"Is that Rachel's handwriting?"

"I didn't see much of it, but I suspect it is. It's interesting. The signatures don't line up, and they don't look … fluent, I guess you'd say. Like somebody was practicing somebody else's signature."

"Rachel pretending to be Tiffany Cobb."

"Which is why her blonde wig was gone."

"We really need to find her," said Drake.

"The mainland is pretty big. So they tell me."

Agnes checked her phone. No bars. That still happened frequently on this island. Drake caught her expression and started toward the car before she said a word.

Back on the blacktop Drake got a signal. Agnes fed him Lanny's number. When Lanny answered, Drake put him on speaker. Before Agnes could speak, Lanny broke in.

"Coutinho is down at Kalapana. Seems a body just washed ashore. Female."

Agnes didn't ask how he knew. Lanny guarded his police sources zealously, even from her.

"Haven't been any missing persons that I heard of," he said.

And the island might be big, but the population was small. One suspicious death was a lot. The odds were high that this dead woman had something to do with the case.

"Meet us there," she told him.

She turned to Drake.

"It's a short trip."

But as she drove, she realized that it might still look long to a visitor who was used to New Jersey. The first leg of the trip, to Pahoa, the unofficial capital of the Puna district, felt like just another errand, but the rest of the trip to Kalapana seemed longer. Traffic was sparse. A mainland friend had once told Agnes, "I kept going, but nobody was coming back. So I'm wondering, is the earth swallowing everybody up, or are they smart enough not to go in the first place?"

The lava at Kalapana didn't care about the tourism industry on the island. It flowed, or it didn't. When it put on a show, traffic picked up, but mostly at night, when the views were most spectacular. But now, in the middle of the day, Agnes and Drake saw almost no one until they passed the barrier where years earlier a lava flow had cut across Highway 130. Agnes parked where the lava enthusiasts got out to walk the rest of the way to the ocean. Twenty years of local traffic had smoothed the lava somewhat, but Agnes still watched her footing.

As she and Drake approached the ocean, they saw several mismatched vehicles parked at odd angles. One was an official Hawaii County Police van, and there was an ambulance next to it. Blue cones marked the rest as the personal vehicles of police personnel.

Officer Freitas was controlling the scene. Agnes approached, expecting the officer to send her back to her Camry. Instead, Freitas nodded her onward. Drake followed. Agnes looked back in time to catch Freitas stealing a look at him.

The young officer had good taste in men. If Agnes ever felt like trying the female bonding thing, she might pick Freitas.

Coutinho was standing on a flat black volcanic rock. Another step would have pitched him into the surf ten feet below him, and the Portuguese fatalism that always draped itself over him almost made Agnes worry for a moment.

"Don't jump," she said as she stopped at his elbow.

She bent forward to see what had absorbed his attention in the surf below. All she saw was boiling surf of a sullen gray that mirrored the sky.

"Wasn't planning to."

"What's so fascinating?"

"That's where we pulled her out."

"Who?"

"I'm hoping you can help us with that."

She had been dreading that. Perhaps to put the task off, she asked, "Who found her?"

"A local getting some fishing in."

Coutinho waved inland, where new-looking houses sat on the huge field of black rock left by the eruption of 1990. Defiant residents had returned and rebuilt on the land that they still owned. The houses always reminded Agnes of mushrooms.

"Doesn't mean she went in here, though. We'll have to ask somebody at the university about the currents."

He started walking toward the ambulance. She followed. In the back of the vehicle a stretcher had a covered form strapped onto it. Coutinho knew enough to let Agnes climb into the ambulance without help from him. An EMT, a young man of mostly Japanese descent, waited for a signal from Coutinho before uncovering the face.

18

THE BODY HADN'T BEEN in the water long. Agnes had seen longterm floaters. This wasn't as bad, but it was bad enough. This woman should have been good for many more years.

"Not Rachel Park," said Agnes.

"Rachel? How is she involved?"

"You don't know? Oh, right. You and Baclan and Perez don't exactly take coffee breaks together."

As soon as the words left her mouth, Agnes wanted them back. It was a sad state of affairs when being an honest cop was a disadvantage.

"It must be Tiffany Cobb," she said, as a kind of apology.

"Where is Rachel?"

"On the mainland, I'm guessing. Probably traveling as Tiffany Cobb."

"The idea being to make us think Cobb wasn't our problem anymore."

"Which leads to a question."

"Who cared enough about Tiffany Cobb to make her dead?"

Coutinho frowned.

"I guess I need to alert the FBI. I'm sure they'll have a whole lot of time for some cop from Hawaii."

Agnes knew what he meant. Many mainlanders thought Hawaii was a foreign country, although the FBI should know better. She thought Diana Andrews might have a way of shortening the search, but she kept that idea to herself.

And while she got Andrews to do her thing, Agnes needed to find something to get her fingernails under. What occurred to her was a complete workup of Marci Savage. If her death wasn't the result of marital troubles, what else might someone have had against her?

"Thanks for coming out, Counselor."

"I hesitate to say, 'Anytime.'"

"I know what you mean."

This was getting too weird. If she didn't get away from him right now, they might start exchanging Christmas cards.

Agnes checked her phone, but Kalapana was another place on the island where cell phone coverage was still iffy. She started driving toward Pahoa. As she passed the turnoff for the town, her ring tone startled her. She pulled over to the shoulder. She didn't believe in talking and driving, but it was more than that. Local cops who wouldn't bother another motorist would make a point of busting her.

"I need to come clean with you," said Don Savage.

"Where are you?"

"I'm headed your way. I'll hit Na'alehu in a few minutes."

"Get a table in Punalu'u."

"Malasadas," said Savage. "You're revealing a serious weakness."

"I'm not going to eat them. Just admire them, and maybe sniff them a little."

"Uh huh."

That was her second banter session with a cop today. What was wrong with her?

19

AND WITHOUT THINKING she had committed herself to another drive. The southern tip of the island was a good two hours away.

A bus load of Japanese tourists was loading up at the Punalu'u Bake Shop as she and Drake arrived. Like many visitors, they seemed to think the traffic in paradise was as gentle as the weather. Agnes entered the parking lot at five miles an hour, ready for someone to wander into her path.

But she parked without incident. Savage had taken an outdoor table in the Japanese rock garden. He had talked someone into lending him a coffee thermos, and Agnes would have bet that the half dozen donuts were also on the house. Cups sat ready for her and Drake. She poured and studied Savage.

"Where's Tulla? She's supposed to be working for me."

"She is. I told her she needed to tend to her responsibilities."

That told Agnes volumes. How many times in her life had Tulla obeyed a man, even when he was right?

"She's with your principal."

"What brings you down this way?" Agnes asked.

The southern tip of the island was remote even by Big Island standards.

"Just checking in. My wife loved it down here."

Savage sipped coffee.

"I could have told you that part on the phone. The rest needed to be face to face."

Whatever the revelation was, she expected Savage to get right to it. That was his style.

"My wife," said Don Savage, "was a hooker."

20

AGNES SAT BACK and pondered her lack of surprise. This was major, and it had not come out in the trial. Savage read her mind.

"I did a lot of work on hiding her past," he said.

"How was that even possible?"

"It helped that she didn't do it for long, and she never took a bust. Plus, she wasn't kama'aina. Nobody knew anything about her here."

"Where was she from?"

"New Jersey."

When had New Jersey become the center of the universe? Everything kept going back there.

"I met her at a conference in Atlantic City."

"Police stuff?"

"Counter-terrorism. Why Atlantic City, I never found out. Probably somebody high up just wanted to go there."

"So she was hooking."

"I called an escort agency, and they sent her. I had known a lot of hookers, and she had known a fair number of johns. Meaning, we cut through the bullshit. It was real, and we knew it."

His eyes turned inward.

"Almost ten years ago."

"What went wrong?"

"Women have a term for guys like me. I'm a dog. I knew I had it good at home, but that didn't stop me."

Agnes opened her mouth, but then she realized she was about to warn him about doing the same thing to Tulla. That wasn't her business. But then the silence grew, until Agnes realized that she would have to be the one to break it.

"So, when you met Marci, you cleaned up her record."

"A local cop owned a piece of her, but I worked that out with him. He even pulled the contact cards from their files."

Agnes knew about contact cards. They recorded encounters between police and civilians that fell short of an arrest.

He gave her a bleak smile.

"A professional courtesy. I believe lawyers know the term."

"I need to know, Don. What were you and Marci doing on the Hilo side?"

"Paying off a blackmailer."

"About her past?"

"Yeah."

"Who cares these days?"

"I'm kama'aina. I mean, all the way back Most of my family, they think it's still 1819."

The year the first missionaries came to the islands.

"In the ohana network I'm just hanging on by my fingernails as it is. A hooker for a wife? They'd never talk to me again."

Agnes stopped herself from saying, "Is that bad?" In Hawaii family was everything. Most people weren't like her.

"Who was blackmailing you?"

"Good question."

"And you're sure it was Marci's past that was the issue?"

"Pay up, or everybody will know what my wife used to do."

"That's pretty clear."

She looked at him and thought back to their confrontation in the courtroom.

"Now I need to know what really happened that night."

"I recall telling you that. In public."

"I know what you said on the stand, but it makes no sense. You're driving through the rain at five miles an hour, and the window shatters with no warning."

"That's what happened."

"Pretty stupid blackmailer."

"Pretty obvious that it wasn't the blackmailer. Which is why I really believed it was your client."

"Because of that time you beat the shit out of him."

"There was in internal affairs inquiry that found no misconduct."

"As if they ever would."

"You can believe it or not, but it was a real investigation. Not just a rubber stamp. The problem is, some guys in Hank's position, when they realize they're not going to get payback from the system, they decide to handle it themselves."

And Hank had put himself in the frame by wandering around the rainforest with no good explanation. At the same time, the prosecution had never managed to connect the dots. How had Hank known where to look for Don and Marci? How had he penetrated miles into the jungle without a vehicle?

"What I'm thinking now," said Savage, "is a bait and switch. Whoever was supposedly blackmailing us was really out to kill Marci."

"Marci?"

"The demand was texted to her phone."

"What was the exact wording?"

"Bring ten thousand in cash to the eight-mile marker. Don't tell your husband."

"As if they were assuming she would come alone. Which implies less than perfect knowledge about you and Marci. They thought you didn't know about her past."

"That's one possibility."

"But you did know from the beginning. She told you about the blackmail, and you went together."

It just wasn't hanging together. What had the blackmailer really wanted? Agnes needed to know more, and she couldn't think of anyone but the blackmailer who could tell her.

Drake had his cell phone out.

"Check-in time with Tulla," he said.

He punched in numbers. Agnes wondered why he didn't have Tulla on speed dial, but then she realized that it was probably a security measure. If the bad guys got hold of Drake, they couldn't lure his partner into a trap. And Agnes knew he would never give Tulla up.

"Voicemail," he said.

He didn't leave a message, and Agnes watched him delete the number.

But then his cell rang. He answered, and what he heard made him put the caller on speaker.

"I'm kind of busy," said Tulla. "Nothing's happening at the moment, but it will."

"What, exactly?"

"They've got me pinned down. I make it two shooters."

The woman could have been discussing a kitchen renovation. Agnes knew she had more than her own share of grit, but Tulla made her feel inadequate.

"Where are you?" said Drake in the same tone.

"Cole's place. Up where the first shooting happened."

It wasn't the moment to ask Tulla why she had gone there of all places, but Tulla answered the unspoken question.

"Thomas Hanbun called the principal at the resort. Whatever he said got Hank to go up there."

Agnes heard a gunshot, and then another much closer report. Tulla must have returned fire.

"I caught up with him. I assume he's the target."

"Tulla," said Agnes, "we're about as far away from you as we can be."

"I figured."

Tulla fired again. "Anything you can think of will be appreciated."

Agnes took her own phone out and scrolled through the recents. There it was. It might be a futile call, or Thomas might be confused enough to answer.

He did.

"Thomas, stop shooting. Don't make it worse."

He breathed in her ear.

"I know you're involved in this mess. Let me talk to Katie."

Nothing came over the phone. Since that included no gunshots, that was good.

"You're a pain in the ass."

21

THE NEW VOICE WAS FEMALE.

"So they tell me," said Agnes. "What's your plan?"

No answer, but no mayhem.

"Whatever it is, it's falling apart. First rule when you're in a hole. Stop digging. Or in this case, stop shooting."

"I've got nothing to lose now."

"There's always something to lose. If you stop now, a lawyer has something to work with. Who knows whether the cops can make a case for Tiffany Cobb?"

Agnes heard an intake of breath. She decided to press harder.

"Her body floated. Everybody knows she's dead, and it's Rachel Park pretending to be her on the mainland."

"So what do I do?"

The question left Agnes with her mouth hanging open. The woman's actions had seemed so decisive, so ruthless, until now.

"I work for the system. You know that. I have to tell you to come in and let the system work."

"I need a lawyer."

"You're right about that. It can't be me, but I can get you somebody good."

The silence stretched. Every second without shooting was progress, but it couldn't go on like this forever. Agnes opened her mouth to keep her connection with the woman going, but she had no idea what she was going to say.

"Speaking of names, what's yours?"

"Orozco."

"Kama'aina?"

"Yeah. What do you care?"

"Just trying to understand where you're coming from."

"Fuck it," said Orozco. "This is bullshit."

Agnes wondered what else she could say.

Then the gun fired inches from the phone. Agnes flinched as if she had taken the bullet herself.

22

"KATIE?"

No one replied. Agnes and Drake listened for what seemed hours, although she knew it was seconds.

"Call Tulla back."

Drake nodded.

"You guys okay?" Agnes asked.

"Yeah. Things just went quiet."

"Somebody got shot, I think. Sit tight. We'll call nine-one-one."

"Got it."

Agnes was glad she wasn't the one on the spot. She knew that she would have had a hard time resisting the temptation to go see who needed medical attention, but Tulla knew her job. Even if someone bled to death ten feet away, she would protect the principal.

Drake was already making the call. He made a concise

report to the emergency operator as he and Savage followed Agnes toward the parking lot.

It was the most nerve-wracking Big Island drive she had ever made. In her Camry she and Drake said nothing the entire time. Anything would have been speculation. Savage followed in his Avalon. Agnes could only imagine what he was thinking.

Agnes willed her cell phone to ring, even though she knew the cops would keep Tulla too busy to call.

The gate to the Hanbun ranch stood open, which was something Agnes had never seen before. The first thing she saw on the property was an Impala with a blue cone on the roof.

Cops on Cole's land for the second time in days.

A uniformed officer climbed out and held up his palm. Agnes came to a stop beside him.

"Detective Coutinho says to go to the house."

Agnes didn't bother with questions. No one but Coutinho would tell her anything.

An ambulance passed her on its way to the public road. She tried to stop herself from speculating on who was in it, but it was impossible.

And there was the house, with Coutinho standing on the front porch. Agnes parked and climbed out.

"Who was that?" she asked.

"Thomas Hanbun. He says he didn't see who shot him."

"He's an idiot. Katie Orozco shot him."

"How do you know her name?"

"She told me. Why would he protect her?"

"He might think he's protecting his own ass."

"I don't suppose she's still around?"

"No. She's gone, and so is one of the ranch vehicles. A Wrangler."

Meaning Orozco wouldn't be limited to the roads.

"I'm calling a helicopter out. My lieutenant is going to be very pleased."

"The brass always love it when you bust their budget," said Agnes.

If they kept up this cordiality, Coutinho might stop visiting her nighttime fantasies.

"I think it's pretty clear that she killed Tiffany Cobb," Agnes said. "And Marci Savage."

"That's a leap. But anything is possible."

"Motive would help."

"Maybe Thomas can help us with that."

Coutinho gave her a serious look.

"Are you still representing him?"

"I don't think I can. Not if I'm with Hank Alves."

She hated the words as she said them. She was cutting herself off from the case. But there was no help for it.

"Speaking of Hank. Where is he?"

"The bunkhouse."

23

BUT BEFORE AGNES WENT to her client, she had a courtesy call
to make. She knew where to find Cole Hanbun. His study
was his refuge from the chaos around him.

She knocked but heard nothing. She pushed the heavy,
carved wooden door open.

"Cole?"

He was sitting behind his desk. He made no sign that he
had heard her.

"Cole, I'm so sorry. This is my fault."

He sat like a statue.

"I'd like to say I'll make it up to you, but I don't make
promises I can't keep. I won't bother you again, though."

She got up to go.

"It's not your fault."

"Yes, it is."

"The government would have come for me sooner or

later. They always come for the true patriots."

Agnes felt a small flare-up of hope. Maybe she hadn't destroyed him. She put her hand over his for a moment and left.

Hank and Tulla were both sitting at the plain wooden table in the bunkhouse. Jenny Freitas stood against the wall, controlling the scene.

One look told Agnes everything. Hank was going to be at his petulant worst. Tulla showed nothing, which struck Agnes as superhuman.

But then Tulla looked right past her and smiled that smile. Agnes knew without looking that Don Savage had followed her. An unwelcoming look from Freitas confirmed it.

"I'll wait," he said.

The two words shut out everyone else in the world.

"Okay," said Tulla.

Don obviously knew that Coutinho didn't want him in his crime scene.

Agnes called Lanny.

"Something else for you to do, since you're relaxing."

"Right."

Agnes knew that tone. Lanny enjoyed feeling overworked and under-appreciated. The key to getting his best work was feeding his complex.

"Keep an ear open for the police frequencies. A helicopter might be spotting a Jeep Wrangler any minute."

"A Wrangler. Now there's something you don't see every day."

If anything gave Katie Orozco a chance of evading capture, it was blending in with the countless Wranglers on this rugged island.

And now that Agnes had a moment to sit and think, she couldn't come up with a better plan than getting everyone to

Hilo and waiting.

It took a while for the cops to get finished with Hank and Tulla. That made four in Agnes's Camry, which was a first. She decided not to think right now about the shortage of people in her life who would ride with her without somebody getting paid to do it. Savage followed again.

24

WHEN SHE HAD EVERYONE in her office, she started thinking aloud.

"We still need you," she said to Drake and Tulla. "I thought you might be done, if the cops weren't coming after Hank anymore. But it wasn't them, and as long as Orozco is out there ..."

"Is she the one gunning for Hank?" said Don Savage.

"I guess, although I can't find her motive. Maybe the cops can get it from Thomas Hanbun."

"Did she kill Marci?"

"I think so. When we finally get a look at her, Hank will know whether she's the hooker he met in the bar. Even if she isn't, she still might be the one who's behind it. She recruited Rachel Park. She must know other women."

"You know," said Savage, "I won't know until I see her, but Orozco might a hooker I busted. Modesty? I think that's what she called herself."

"You busted her? There's an actual arrest record? Or did you take a freebie and her earnings for the day?"

Savage said nothing. Agnes glanced at Tulla and saw the woman adding it up. The sum was apparently something she could live with.

"How much did you get from her?"

"Fifteen hundred."

To Agnes that sounded like at least three dates. She tried to imagine spreading her legs for three unpleasant or downright repulsive men and then watching a fourth man pocketing her payday.

"So here's a hooker with a grudge against you."

"I guess."

What filled the silence was her cell phone, with the ring tone that said Lanny needed her attention.

"The cops have the Wrangler," he said. "Up by Hawi."

Agnes pictured the map of the northern tip of the island. A short off-road trip of the kind that the Wrangler was designed for would have put Orozco on Highway 200, which would have given her a straight shot to the tiny town.

"Was she in it?"

"Doesn't sound like it."

"I'll bet she just got out and caught a ride."

Hardbitten mainlanders often didn't understand the open, trusting nature of Big Island residents. Many people who saw a woman hitchhiking would have stopped without hesitation or ulterior motives.

"Meaning she could be anywhere."

Agnes realized that she was thumbing numbers into her cell phone. When she looked at the digits on the screen, she further realized that she hadn't considered the time difference. It was close to midnight in New Jersey, but the voice that answered sounded alert.

"Diana Andrews."

Agnes filled her in. She could feel Andrews thinking.

"Let me make some calls."

"I'll owe you big time."

"You have my people. I want them back. Preferably the way you got them."

And now Agnes couldn't think of any place to go but home, which brought her face to face with the strangeness of her life. She liked her home. She might even love it, but going there always took an effort of will. It was a haven, but that was also a problem. Nothing ever happened there, and sometimes the silence unnerved her.

She knew one person on the island who would understand. This huge island had the population of a medium sized city, and it was sometimes hard not to hear about people's business. She knew that Coutinho had lived alone for two years between marriages to his wife Lucy.

But she couldn't discuss the single life with him for any number of reasons.

There was nothing to do but start driving again.

25

HER CELL PHONE RANG, making her flinch and at the same time thank the god of work. She recognized the number and pulled over to the shoulder.

"Got something for you," said Diana Andrews.

"I can sure use something."

"Katie Orozco. She's one of my tribe. My former tribe, I mean."

"That's interesting."

"Maybe even more than you know. She's hard core. Full-time professional prostitute, travels the nationwide circuit. East coast to Honolulu and back, a week at a time in major cities. For her purposes Atlantic City counts as major."

"What else?"

"Several professional names, but the most recent is Modesty."

"Adorable. How did you find out about her?"

"I can't give you much detail, but Roy was plugged into counterintelligence circles."

Agnes knew that Roy Litvinov was the deceased founder of the security firm that Andrews now led.

"Some of those people still feel they owe him. Seems Katie Orozco came onto their radar, because some of her clients are the kind of people these people keep an eye on. The kind who do things for the government that other countries would like to know about."

"Making them a security risk. Blackmail?"

"Getting caught with a hooker isn't that much of an embarrassment anymore. But pillow talk is the same problem it always was."

Andrews paused.

"From there I called a cop I know in Atlantic City. From my old career."

"I would guess he was surprised to hear from you."

"She. Name is Novotny. She was surprised enough to let some interesting stuff slip about Orozco."

"The cops knew her."

"Cops always know who's doing that kind of work. Some of them view it as a profit center."

"Payoffs."

"Most women learn to look at it as a cost of doing business. Orozco didn't. She pushed back. It got so she wasn't welcome there anymore."

"How has she lasted so long in the business?"

"Well, it looks as if she may have snapped. I've known it to happen."

"Did you get anything on Tiffany Cobb?"

"No, but it would stand to reason."

Another pause.

"One thing about my old line of work. Some guys hired

me for things that were only slightly related to sex, if at all."

"Such as blackmail."

"I wouldn't have dug myself that kind of hole, but some women were pretty reckless if the money was good enough. You know …"

"What?"

"You have two suspects. That could mean two motives."

"Blackmail for one and murder for the other."

"And the way it played out, I would guess that Tiffany Cobb was the blackmailer. Somehow, she knew about Marci Savage. Maybe from Atlantic City. Orozco used Cobb to get Don Savage out in the open where she wanted him."

"And then she didn't need Tiffany anymore. No, it's worse. She couldn't afford to let her live."

"I'll try to nail it down, whether Tiffany Cobb had a New Jersey connection."

"There's also the question, whether Katie was really shooting at Marci or Don."

"Find her and ask her."

26

ANDREWS DISCONNECTED, leaving Agnes to think. It was hanging together, even Rachel's survival. Orozco needed her alive for now to pose as Tiffany, but if Agnes had been Rachel, she would have made herself hard to find. She hoped Rachel was smart enough to figure that out.

The phone rang again. Agnes looked at the display. She didn't recognize the number, which was local. This was the number on her business card, which meant it might even be a job with a retainer. It might be time to get back to paying work. She answered.

"Agnes?"

It was an unfamiliar number, but Agnes knew the voice.

"Rachel, where are you?"

"I'm home."

"Did Katie Orozco give you a new phone?"

"How do you know Katie?"

"We need to talk about that."

Agnes decided to say nothing more over the airwaves.

"Stay there."

It was a risk, but she probably had a head start on Orozco, wherever the woman was headed. Unfortunately, if Orozco knew Rachel was back, her home was the obvious place to look for her. When it came to eliminating witnesses, Katie Orozco had decided to err on the side of murder.

And now Agnes had an idea what was driving the woman. Don Savage had been one shakedown too many.

This time the trip disappeared without her noticing. Agnes felt the mud slipping and sliding under her wheels and realized that she had left Hilo behind.

Rachel's place appeared on the right. Agnes slowed enough to avoid kicking mud at the house when her brakes bit. Rachel appeared in the doorway. Agnes sent her passenger window down.

"Get in, Rachel. We need to get out of here."

Rachel gave her an uncomprehending look.

"Katie Orozco is on her way here. You don't want her to find you."

"Why not?"

"Rachel, get in."

Agnes put a whiplash into her voice, and it finally got the other woman moving. Agnes started a U-turn and had a bad moment when the right front wheel spun. But the left got enough traction to complete the turn. She started driving back toward Hilo.

"Tell me if I have this right," said Agnes. "Katie Orozco paid you to go to the mainland."

"No."

"No?"

Could Agnes have this all wrong?

"I told Katie I needed to see my sister in Vegas, and she lent me the money."

"Did you tell her how long you'd be away?"

"I told her two weeks, but me and my sister kinda had a beef. I'm back early."

"But you were supposed to pretend to be Tiffany."

"I am Tiffany. For business."

It was like pulling teeth.

"But Katie wanted me to wear my blonde wig."

"Did she say why?"

"No."

That was the Rachel Agnes knew. Her lack of curiosity about anything that wasn't right in front of her could be good or bad.

But she had said enough to confirm Agnes's theory.

"Why do I have to come with you?"

"To keep Katie from killing you."

Rachel gaped, and Agnes could see that she was unable to process the information.

"Shit," said Agnes.

Up ahead an elderly Crown Victoria had skidded sideways in the mud. Its rear wheels had sunk so deep that Agnes knew the car wasn't going anywhere.

Who was stupid enough to take a rear-wheel-drive sedan off the pavement?

Agnes thought she had room to sneak by on the left. Her left front tire floundered in the mud, but this time the right had enough purchase to keep the car going. The shack on the left crowded the road, with only about ten feet of clearance. Agnes glanced as she passed.

Oh, she thought.

Then she ducked, as her side window shattered. Rachel screamed. Agnes floored the gas pedal.

That was a mistake. For an interminable moment the wheels spun. She heard another gunshot. The bullet must have passed through both front side windows without hitting anything.

Finally, the tires bit enough to propel the car forward.

Rachel was still screaming.

"Rachel, stop."

Rachel didn't. Agnes risked taking her right hand off the steering wheel to squeeze Rachel's wrist.

"Stop screaming and listen."

Agnes glanced at the rear-view mirror. A dark colored sport utility vehicle had appeared and was closing in on her car. She could make out long dark hair on the driver.

Katie Orozco? Or a local co-conspirator who could steal a Crown Vic with a few minutes notice? That didn't narrow it down much in this neighborhood.

Agnes shook her head. She didn't have time for this now.

Her cell phone started ringing. She had no time for that, either.

It was going to be close. The pursuer had the advantage in the mud, but the pavement began just ahead. Her Camry had a chance.

The SUV ended up helping. The driver sped up and hit the Camry's rear bumper hard. Agnes fought to control the car, as the added momentum threatened to overwhelm the steering. But that meant the gap between her and the SUV was widening as she bumped onto the blacktop. Now her tires grabbed the road, and she could floor the gas pedal.

As she reached the first of the beaches on the right, she saw people milling in the parking lots. The pursuer must have drawn the same conclusion—that there were too many witnesses now. The SUV turned into one of the parking lots, as if that had been the driver's plan all along.

Agnes was willing to go along with the act. She kept driving into Hilo.

On impulse she turned onto Banyan Drive, where most of the hotels clustered. Rental cars would be thick on the ground, and her Camry would blend in.

Sometimes it seemed to her that hotels were her natural habitat. At the Hilo Hawaiian the desk clerk, a young woman, greeted her. Agnes requested a meeting room. The lobby would be too exposed, if the pursuer's tenacity led her this way.

27

AGNES POINTED RACHEL to a seat at the table in the center of the room and took out her phone. Somehow Agnes knew who had called while she had been saving her own life.

"Bingo," said Diana Andrews. "Tiffany Cobb rang a bell with a contact of mine. She worked the same national escort circuit as Orozco, and Atlantic City was a regular stop. The time frame works."

"I guess Roy Litvinov knew everybody," said Agnes.

"No, this contact was one of mine. From my old life, I mean."

Andrews laughed.

"I forgot. You know her too. Heather from Morristown."

"Does that make me a Jersey girl?"

"Honorary," said Andrews.

"So far your people are in the same condition I got them in."

"Why do I hear a 'But?'"

Agnes told her about Tulla's shootout and the attack on her and Rachel.

"I'm on my way to the airport."

"Oh?" said Agnes.

"I'm coming to you. With reinforcements."

It took a moment for Agnes to process the words.

"To Hawaii?"

"I have to start acting like the boss. I can't send my people to do something I wouldn't do."

"Okay."

"Try to stay alive."

As Agnes disconnected, she realized that she had to make another call. In fact, she should have made it first.

"Coutinho."

"I may have found Katie Orozco."

"How?"

She told him the story.

"How the hell did she get there that fast?"

"I did, so it's possible. Barely."

"It doesn't work if she hitchhiked. She must have had a plan. And people to call on."

"By the way, Diana Andrews is coming."

"Shit."

"What is your problem with her?"

"Leave that for another time. Maybe after we're both retired."

"Well, I need her now."

Coutinho knew how to concentrate on the important stuff.

"I can't put a BOLO out on a dark SUV."

It was like looking for blue in the ocean.

"It occurs to me," said Agnes, "that Thomas Hanbun is

ALBERT TUCHER

in danger. Katie is eliminating complications, which to her could mean just about anybody she knows."

"We have officers on him in the hospital."

"Ask him whether he's the haole who took Rachel Park away. I'm thinking Katie told Thomas to do it."

"I'll ask him if he doesn't lawyer up."

And that told Agnes what she had to do next. The best thing would have been to talk to Thomas, but the police wouldn't let her see him. She no longer represented him. But she knew one person who would talk to her, whereas he would have nothing to say to cops.

It meant another drive. This one she would do alone, with only her thoughts for company. She knew how to do that.

28

"COLE, WHAT HAS THOMAS BEEN UP TO?"

"No drugs. I know what to look for now, and he hasn't been using."

"Okay."

"He had some kind of business plan going."

"Do you know what?"

"No. He kept saying he wanted to get it off the ground first, but that started to get old. I don't think he ever planned to tell me, because I wouldn't approve."

Agnes was getting a glimmer.

"Did he ever have women come up here?"

"Yeah, several. He said they were girlfriends, but they didn't come across like girlfriends. Not the way they looked at him."

Agnes felt her hands itching for a photo of Katie Orozco to show him. Did such a thing exist?

"Was she one of them?"

She showed him the surreptitious snap of Tiffany Cole.

"Yes, I remember her."

"She's a prostitute."

"I can see it. I would suppose the others are, too."

"My guess," said Agnes, "would be that Thomas was starting an escort agency."

Cole received the news without surprise.

"He probably thought he was using them, when they were exploiting him."

"Does the name Katie Orozco ring a bell?"

"No."

"How about Modesty?"

"Not her, either. Is she one of them?"

"I think so. And I think she was seriously sick of being used by men."

"That was probably the wrong line of work for her," said Cole.

"Is there a right one?"

After twenty years of lawyering Agnes usually knew how to clamp down on her urge to blurt, but that one had gotten clean away. Cole didn't seem to notice, though.

"Cole, when you see Thomas, ask him about this. I need to know if we're right about it."

"I guess you can't represent him anymore."

"Not in this. I had to make a choice."

"Sometimes I wish I could."

That left Agnes without much to say. It also reminded her that she needed to check in with her client. She got up and started for the door. If she said goodbye to Cole, he wouldn't hear her.

Outside she stood by her Camry and dialed Drake.

"You have the principal?"

"Of course."

"It's getting worse. I think Katie has help, and I don't even know who you should watch out for. Everybody, I guess."

"We always watch out for everybody."

"I'm on my way to you."

"Then what?"

"Hunker down until Diana gets here, I guess."

29

AGNES DECIDED SOMETHING. When this was over, she planned to treat herself to at least a long weekend of forgetting that she even owned a car.

She pulled into the parking lot at Ken's House of Pancakes. It was somehow fitting. Agnes had first seen Diana Andrews in Rosen's restaurant, five thousand miles away, and thought she could have been in Ken's. Now they were meeting in Ken's. Andrews had a booth for four. Drake and Hank Alves were with her, leaving one empty place for Agnes. She took her seat.

"I'm trying to spot your reinforcements," said Agnes. "Nobody stands out."

"They're here."

"Then they're very good."

"Yes, they are," said Andrews.

"Excuse me a moment while I rip my client a new asshole."

Andrews smiled slightly. Hank flinched.

"Don't ever go off without Tulla or Drake again."

The words were measured, but Agnes put some effort into her glare. Hank looked as if he might be having an incontinent event.

"What did Thomas Hanbun say that got you to go up there?"

Hank looked pathetically grateful that she was letting him live, for the moment.

"He said he had evidence of who killed Marci Savage."

"What kind of evidence?"

"He didn't say. But supposedly he needed me to look it over. Like I had a missing piece of the puzzle."

"That's lame, Hank."

"Yeah, well, I want this to be over."

"There we're in agreement," said Agnes.

"Maybe I can help with that," said Andrews.

"Okay."

"I talked to Heather again. This time she opened up a little more. Seems that Tiffany Cobb talked to her about a prostitutes' organization that somebody was starting. Somebody she had met just recently."

"Like a union?"

"If you can have a union for an illegal business."

"There are precedents," said Agnes.

"I've heard of COYOTE. But this sounded like it at least straddled the line between advocacy and extortion."

"And that sounds like our Katie."

"There's precedent for that, too. It's not news that some unions have made questionable alliances. They felt they had no choice against powerful opponents."

"You're not sounding very corporate right now."

"I'm an imposter," said Andrews. "I feel like a fraud every

time I go into that office with 'President' on the door. Someday they're going to realize, and I'll be out of a job."

"Who's 'they?'"

"Ask Cole Hanbun. The same 'they' he's always ranting about."

"You've Googled him."

"He has quite a presence online. I could have spent days tracking him through the conspiracy blogs."

"This hangs together," said Agnes. "I was wondering how Katie Orozco got to Hilo from North Kohala so fast. Maybe it wasn't Katie."

"Somebody from her hooker posse."

"And maybe we're up against a whole bunch of pissed-off women."

"You did tell us to watch out for everyone," said Drake.

Agnes gave him a sharp look, but he maintained his bland façade.

Andrews looked around.

"This place hasn't changed."

"There would be a riot if it ever did."

"I even recognize some of the waitresses," said Andrews.

A Filipino-Japanese beauty who would have caused male whiplash injuries anywhere in the world brushed by their table. Here she was a waitress.

"She's new, though."

"I worked here for a while," said Agnes. "Two college summers, Ninety-four and Ninety-five."

"I had been hooking for almost ten years at that point."

"Maybe I should have tried it. I was giving it away to older men anyway, and making peanuts pouring coffee."

"Which was exactly my thinking at the time."

Agnes blinked. This was almost as weird as bonding with Coutinho.

Andrews tapped on the table with her index finger.

"I think we need to press the issue. We need to finish this, or you'll be looking over your shoulder forever."

"Plus, you want your people back."

"There's that. I'm getting paid for this, but I can't keep turning down other business."

"So how do we flush them out?"

"Show me where that SUV attacked. We think there's somebody down that way who's in it with Katie Orozco. We can make sure we're seen, and hope we draw them out."

The beautiful young waitress passed again. Agnes slid out of the booth and waited for everyone to join her.

30

OUT IN THE PARKING LOT Agnes looked around. She still couldn't pick out the new bodyguards Andrews.

"I don't think we need to make the detour," said Andrews.

"Why not?"

"That waitress is probably dropping a dime on us right now."

"You got a vibe from her."

"I did. She's a natural for my old line of work. She has the looks, and she needs more money than she makes here."

"So maybe she's in with Katie."

"Where's a good place to make this happen?"

"The Saddle Road," said Agnes. "Usually nobody around, no collateral damage."

"That's good. It's also a plausible route to Cole Hanbun's place. We can pretend we're oblivious."

"I keep forgetting you know this island," said Agnes. "Wait

a minute. We're going to get there ahead of your people."

"I sent them on ahead. I figured north. Let me tell them where to link up with us."

Andrews got on her cell phone and gave some terse instructions.

"Let's go."

The four of them went outside. As they approached the Camry, a man fell into step alongside the party. He took Hank's elbow and drew him aside to a forgettable rented Nissan Sentra. A second man appeared. Agnes had to stop herself from doing a double take. The second man was the same size and coloring as Hank Alves, and his blue polo shirt and khaki pants were identical to Hank's. The same man held out his hand. Agnes gave him her keys with a mental shrug. If she was going to hire experts, she should listen to them.

Without breaking step, the new man climbed into the Camry with Agnes, Andrews and Drake. The car started and merged onto 19. The driver knew the turns to the Saddle Road.

Agnes tried to get used to riding in the back seat of her own car. Having Diana Andrews to her left increased the novelty of the situation.

After about ten minutes of silence Andrews said, "This is the third time this island is trying to kill me."

"Let's not let that happen," said Agnes after a moment.

She tried not to cringe at how lame she sounded.

Barbed wire fences and the occasional gate began to appear on both sides of the road. This was the southern edge of cattle country.

Up ahead the trail to Hairy Hill came into view, with its tangled, bristly vegetation suggesting an unkempt beard. All her life Agnes had been driving past the place and telling herself to do the tourist thing and climb the hill for its views.

Three sedans with the look of rental cars were parked along the shoulder.

"Those your people?" said Agnes.

"Yes. I told them to park like visitors."

"It fits. Any vehicles that aren't yours?"

"No, we're good."

Agnes drove the Saddle Road often enough to have it imprinted in her mind. Sometimes it was the most direct route, and sometimes she just felt like skipping all the reduced speed zones of the northern and southern routes around the island.

So she knew when something was different. But what?

And it hit her. One of the cattle gates that lined the road stood open. She had never seen that gate open.

31

AND AS THE FACT REGISTERED, so did the roar of engines.

Plural. More than one. More than two.

Three Wranglers powered over a ridge that had concealed them on ranch land. The first one came through the open gate and aimed right at the Camry. Seconds before it crushed the right side of the car, the driver floored the accelerator. The car paused for an agonizing instant and then leaped ahead.

Instead of crushing Drake in the passenger seat, the Wrangler slammed into the right rear of the Camry and spun the car around.

"Reverse," said Andrews in a tone that struck Agnes as dementedly calm. Agnes decided to let her handle it. If someone could keep thinking in this situation, she was fine with that. The driver wrenched the lever into reverse and floored the gas pedal again. The car kept traveling in its original direction, only backwards.

The other two Wranglers gained the surface of the highway and came after the Camry. Agnes saw that Andrews had produced a handgun from somewhere. Agnes knew a Glock when she saw one. She had shot Glocks herself. A glance in the mirror told her that Drake was also holding a pistol. The driver found time to send all the windows down. It seemed to take ages for the glass to get out of the way of the guns.

Andrews reached across Agnes and put two shots into the lead Wrangler. Agnes had no time to see whether the bullets hit anyone. The Wrangler swerved off the road into the ditch. The driver put the car in Drive and floored the pedal. The Camry took off toward Hilo.

The driver of the last Wrangler had more nerve. The vehicle kept coming. This time the Camry swerved to get by, but there wasn't enough pavement for the tires to grip. The car shot off the road into the ditch.

"Out," said Andrews.

Her conversational tone helped Agnes get out of her seat belt with an efficiency that amazed her even as she did it. Agnes tumbled from the car into the ditch. She rolled over. Things looked bad. Andrews and the two men were taking cover behind the Camry. Agnes made a mental note to start researching new cars. Then she told herself to focus on essentials, such as not dying.

Then three women jumped out of the Wrangler in the ditch. They had clear shots at Agnes and her team.

Andrews looked unconcerned, and Agnes wanted to scream at her to do something. But then the Wrangler shuddered from a tremendous impact. The three women understood a moment before Agnes. They dropped their handguns and raised their hands.

A hundred yards away, Tulla stood by the cluster of

vehicles parked by the Hairy Hill turnoff. She held a rifle ready for another shot, if it proved necessary.

That's a big fucking gun, Agnes thought with a touch of ridiculous pride.

Who was she to be proud of Tulla?

Silence fell.

Andrews and the two men didn't need words to divide up the task of clearing the three Wranglers out. In minutes they had eight women lined up and kneeling on the stiff brown grass by the side of the highway. Agnes felt a moment of sympathy for the women's knees, but she pushed it away. She looked at the prostitutes, because that was what they must be.

She saw a cross-section of female humanity—every hue from Scandinavian blonde through the various Pacific rim colorings to one dark-complected black woman.

Drake and the other man were busy rooting in the Wranglers and making a pile of the guns they found there. Andrews walked from one end of the line of women to the other.

"Who's Katie Orozco?"

No one spoke.

"If one of you is Katie, you need to do the right thing and take the weight. You got these girls into this."

Nothing.

"Okay, somebody give her up. First one gets the good deal."

No one moved.

"Okay, you're right. I'm not a cop, but I know how they do things. How do I know? Take a guess."

Still nothing.

"I'm one of you. That's right. I was in the life for fourteen years, and I'm telling you. Solidarity is great. I admire it. I

115

wish we had more of it back then. But solidarity has to go both ways. If it stops, you need to look out for number one. Katie is hanging you out to dry."

The black woman stood.

"Nobody told you to get up," said Drake.

"I'm Katie," said the woman.

"No, I am."

That was the pale blonde.

"No, I am."

"I am."

"I am."

"Spartacus," said Agnes.

Drake gave her a blank look. Was she really that much older, or was he just too busy for movies?

She glanced ahead and saw that Tulla was still in position, just in case another shot was needed. Agnes sidled closer to Andrews.

"I don't think we can put off calling Coutinho much longer."

"Go ahead. Orozco isn't here."

"She must have a real hold on these women, if she can give them a mission like this and trust them to go through with it. And volunteer to do her time for her."

"She pressed the right buttons. We all have them. She found them."

32

COUTINHO ANSWERED HIS CELL. He always did. Agnes caught herself wondering again whether he was ever off duty, and what his wife thought about that. Agnes had never met Lucy Coutinho and didn't think she ever wanted to.

"We have nine-one-one for this," he said.

"I'm notifying the police. Which is you."

"Sit tight."

Everyone waited, but Andrews and Drake were good at it. It stood to reason. Body guarding involved a lot of mindful waiting. No one but Agnes seemed to feel a need to speak. She realized she would be talking just to fill the silence, and she mastered the urge.

When the first Hawaii County Police cone appeared on top of another Camry, Andrews and her people set their firearms down on the ground and stepped away from them.

Coutinho climbed out of the Camry. Agnes found

herself watching Diana Andrews, whose expression revealed nothing.

"Aloha," said Coutinho.

He could have loaded the word with sarcasm, but he didn't. It was another thing to admire about him, not that Agnes would ever admit it.

"Thank you, Detective," said Andrews. "It's been a while."

It was an opening for Coutinho to reply, "Not long enough," but again he passed.

A Malibu that Agnes recognized as Jenny Freitas's personal vehicle parked behind Coutinho's Camry. Freitas and a young man in uniform emerged. Behind them an official Hawaii County Ford SUV also slowed and parked. The cops would need it to transport their prisoners.

Coutinho surveyed the women lined up by the highway.

"You're making me feel young again."

Agnes gave him a blank look.

"Back in my uniform days I did a few prostitution sweeps. Detectives don't do much of that. Never mind. Which one is Orozco?"

"None of them," said Agnes.

Coutinho nodded. He didn't ask her whether she was sure. That was another good thing about him.

"We'll need statements from all of you."

"We'll see you in Hilo," said Agnes.

33

"THIS PLACE LOOKS LIKE A FORT," said Andrews.

She had followed Agnes to her car in the visitors' lot at Hawaii County Police headquarters.

"Do they really expect a military assault?"

"I've told them that," said Agnes. "It doesn't say much for their community relations. Coutinho knows."

Andrews gave her a sideways look.

"He's cute."

"And very married. Which is usually just the way I like them. But it's not happening with a cop."

"My husband is a retired police chief."

"Does he know?"

"About my past? Of course. I lived in his town when I was still in the life. Matter of fact, I was a suspect in the biggest case of his career."

"A murder?"

"Several. And a kidnapping."

Agnes felt stupid for asking. Of course, Bert Jadlowsky knew about Diana's early career. Cops always knew who was selling sex, even when they decided to look the other way.

"You still have some time left on the meter," said Andrews. "And this isn't over."

"Who is this angel who's paying my bills for me?"

"I can't tell you his name. But I solved his daughter's murder."

"In which life?"

"The old one. Because of something only a hooker would know."

Agnes wondered what else to ask, while Andrews was in a sharing mood.

But then she got a look on her face that Agnes had never expected to see. Andrews looked dumbfounded. On top of the look came the brutal crack of a gunshot. She stumbled forward. Agnes caught her in an embrace, and then the other woman's weight began to drag them both down.

That was just as well. Another bullet pounded into the door of the car just above them. Andrews settled on top of Agnes in a way that felt familiar, or would have if the other woman had been a man.

Another time, Agnes thought.

She rolled Andrews off her with a mental apology for the roughness. High up on the right side of Diana's chest a patch of red had blossomed. It spread rather than pumped, which Agnes knew was not exactly good, but not as bad as it could have been.

She reached toward Andrews and felt around her waist. Her hand found the woman's belt holster, which was empty.

Shit, Agnes thought.

She looked around. A Glock lay on the ground around

six feet away. Andrews must have drawn the weapon instinctively and then lost control of her muscles. Agnes began to crawl toward the Glock. She reached for the weapon, but a shot skittered off the blacktop just ahead of her hand. She backtracked quickly.

She and Andrews must be out of the line of fire as long as they stayed where they were. But how long could they hide?

Think, Agnes told herself.

Diana's handbag lay on the ground by her thigh. Would she have only one gun? Agnes hoped not. She snagged the bag with her hand and fumbled with the clasp. She wrenched the bag open and felt inside it, tentatively, because another woman's bag was her territory.

Idiot, Agnes told herself.

She dumped the contents on the blacktop. There was the item she needed—a small snub-nosed revolver.

Footsteps sounded close by. Agnes picked the gun up and concealed it under her right thigh. She looked up and saw a woman in her thirties. Here was the cause of all the death and destruction, and Katie Orozco looked like just another beautiful island brunette.

"Pretty gutsy," said Agnes. "Or maybe just stupid. You do know this is a police station?"

"Take the fight to the enemy, I always say."

Orozco laughed.

"Actually, I just started saying it recently. It's been interesting."

"I'll bet."

"The cops probably can't believe what they're seeing."

"So you know they have cameras on this lot."

"I have a minute or two. Is she dead?"

"Yes," said Agnes, but she could see that a second's hesitation had cost her crucial credibility with Orozco.

"Let's make sure."

Orozco hefted the rifle and aimed at Diana's head.

"Police," came a familiar voice. "Don't move."

The Camry blocked Agnes's view, but she knew the voice. She had never welcomed Coutinho's input more. Jenny Freitas darted into view, as she attempted to cover open ground and flank Orozco. Katie swung the rifle and snapped off a shot. Freitas stumbled, and Agnes caught herself praying that the young officer was wearing a vest.

And Agnes didn't believe in God.

She heard a shot from a Smith and Wesson Nine. That was Coutinho. Agnes decided that it was time to stop this nonsense. She hoped she had enough firepower. The gun felt small, and the barrel short, and she didn't have time to practice.

Agnes raised the gun. Three pulls at the trigger produced three pops.

Orozco gave her an incredulous look.

"You bitch. You shot me."

She had to take a step away to aim the rifle at Agnes. The Smith sounded twice more, and this time Orozco took on the same dumbfounded look as Diana Andrews and melted to the ground. Agnes stretched out her legs and kicked at Orozco until she rolled over, too far from the rifle to grab it if she had any fight left in her.

It was Freitas who appeared first. Agnes set her gun down on the blacktop and pushed it away. Freitas nodded. She went to Orozco and handcuffed her where she lay.

"You okay?"

"Yes," said Agnes. "You?"

"I'll be hurting tomorrow."

So Freitas was wearing a vest.

"She's not okay," said Agnes.

She rolled the other way and crouched over Diana. Agnes leaned on the wound with both hands.

Hooker blood, she thought. Who knows what's in it?

She felt her face burn with shame. That was one thought she would never confess to anyone.

Freitas got on her radio and started calling for backup and an ambulance.

Coutinho came around the Camry. He went straight to Orozco on the ground and felt for a pulse.

"She's alive. Must be pretty tough."

"I don't care about her," said Agnes.

She kept applying pressure to the wound. Around her the bustle increased, and her mind registered the flashing of emergency lights. Someone pulled her away, while someone else took over the first aid for her.

34

COUTINHO HAD INSISTED on getting her checked out in the hospital. The ER physician was unimpressed with her skinned knees and elbows, and he kicked Agnes out with a few sprays of disinfectant and some Bandaids.

Coutinho met her in the hall.

"Where's Diana?" she asked.

"Come with me."

He started walking her down the hall.

"Who's alive?"

"Katie is," said Coutinho. "Never met a suspect who cared less about the Miranda warning. I couldn't shut her up if I tried."

"She's talking? She's even tougher than I thought."

"You're right about that."

"What is she saying?"

"She killed Marci Savage trying to shoot Don. And she

took both shots at Hank Alves."

"Damn," said Agnes.

"What?"

"I wish I could represent her. What a challenge that would be."

Coutinho left that one alone.

"Here we are."

"You coming in?"

Agnes felt disgusted with herself for hiding behind a man, but she couldn't deny that she wanted him to stay.

But he shook his head.

"I'm not his biggest fan, and he's not mine."

"Who?"

But Coutinho just nodded toward the room and started toward the exit.

There were two men in the room. One was a hell of a seventy-year-old man. Agnes had always had an eye for older men. To her fifty was the sweet spot, but a woman who had chosen this man twenty years earlier would still feel she had done well. He sat by the bed and held Diana's hand in both of his.

"Mr. Jadlowsky? I'm Agnes Rodrigues."

The man looked up. His eyes met hers without giving a hint of what was going on behind them. Agnes felt an urge to babble. That alone would have told her how formidable this man was.

"I'm the one who got her into this."

He shook his head.

"This is what she does. And this is what can happen. Which is not to say you're my favorite person right now, but never mind."

The other man looked less understanding. Agnes waited until Jadlowsky caught on and said, "This is our son, Howard

Pratt."

Agnes caught herself gaping. The young man was thirty-ish, and Diana was several years short of fifty.

"Adopted," said Howard Pratt in a tone that said he had tired of explaining long ago.

Another story that Agnes would have loved to hear.

"Howard," said Jadlowsky, "why don't you and Ms. Rodrigues get some coffee. Then you can spell me here for a while."

So that was how Jadlowsky planned to punish her. He was telling Howard to be civil, but the young man's tolerance would be a lot harder to endure than an outright attack.

Hilo Medical Center was the biggest hospital on the island, but that didn't take much. Agnes knew the way to the coffee shop. It was a short walk, which meant that she wouldn't be able to maintain a polite silence for long.

Howard went to the counter while she chose a table. Agnes was a purist about coffee. She had no patience with decaf or multi-prefixed coffee drinks, which was just as well. She was clearly welcome to keep her preferences to herself.

She took a table and waited. Howard came bearing two cups, which he set down. He seated himself across from her and placed both palms flat. The silence grew.

"She told me that this island had already tried to kill her twice," Agnes heard herself say.

"I didn't want her to go. Neither did Bert."

"But she did."

"You know what worst part is, when she decides to do something that she knows you won't like? She just goes away inside. Like she's gone before she even goes. And she can even do it to us."

"Trying to minimize the hurt, I guess."

"Don't try to get inside her head," said Howard.

Agnes flinched at his tone.

"You don't get to explain her. Not that you could, anyway."

"Can anybody?"

"I'm entitled to try. You aren't."

"Okay."

The silence returned and grew, until Agnes felt that she was about to suffocate.

"My real mother tried to kill her," said Howard.

"Diana?"

"That's who we're talking about, aren't we? And how does she react to that? By adopting me. You'd think she would be nervous about letting me get behind her, but she never was. Like she looked inside me and saw everything there is to see."

Now he was looking inside Agnes, and doing it as well as Bert Jadlowsky. Apparently, Diana was at ease with two men who could do that.

"Diana's the one who steered me toward law school."

"Oh."

"I couldn't get criminal law out of the way fast enough. I don't understand anyone who can do it every day."

"It does take a certain type of person. Which I am, obviously."

Agnes looked at him and realized what she was about to do. He was almost ten years younger, which would usually have been strike one.

"Are you married?" Agnes asked him.

"No. Why?"

Strike two.

"Anybody special?"

And three. He stared.

"No. What's this about?"

Good question, Agnes thought. She usually avoided

single men. But here she was standing and reaching down to coax him to his feet.

She kept holding his hand as she navigated the way out of the building and into the parking lot. She clicked her keyless entry and made the car chirp. She climbed in behind the steering wheel and looked straight ahead as he stared at her. She started the car and waited some more.

He surrendered and got in beside her.

"I live a few blocks away."

"I guess we're going there."

It was ironic. Agnes was habitually neat in her personal habits. Her home was always ready for company, which she seldom had. It was definitely years since a man had entered her front door.

She didn't break her stride as she headed for her bedroom. He was still following her.

"This is how I solve all my problems," she said, as she started unbuttoning her blouse. "And make new ones."

"I was about to say."

But he was keeping up with her, one article of clothing after another.

35

AGNES BROKE THE SILENCE.

"Are you going to tell her about this?"

"Yes.

"Good."

"Good?"

"Because if you don't, I will."

"Why is it so important for her to know?"

Agnes thought about it.

"I guess because kicking my ass gives her something to live for."

"Don't give yourself too much credit. She has lots to live for."

Agnes thought about it.

"I guess she does. We should do this again."

"Welcome to the family," said Howard.

ACKNOWLEDGMENTS

This one is easy. My friend and colleague in all things to do with writing, Elaine Ash aka Anonymous-9, put this book on the right track with her usual efficiency and perceptive-ness. Elaine, thanks as always!

ALBERT TUCHER is the creator of prostitute Diana Andrews, who has appeared in eighty short stories in such venues as Thuglit, Shotgun Honey, and *The Best American Mystery Stories 2010*, edited by Lee Child and Otto Penzler. Diana's first longer case, the novella *The Same Mistake Twice*, was published in 2013. Supporting characters from her world, which includes the Big Island of Hawaii, are featured in *The Place of Refuge*, *The Hollow Vessel*, and *The Honorary Jersey Girl*, all from Shotgun Honey. Albert Tucher recently retired from the Newark Public Library.

On the following pages are a few
more great titles from the
Down & Out Books publishing family.

For a complete list of books and to
sign up for our newsletter,
go to **DownAndOutBooks.com**.

The Place of Refuge
An Errol Coutinho/Big Island of Hawaii Mystery
Albert Tucher

Shotgun Honey, an imprint of
Down & Out Books
978-1-943402-61-8

Detective Errol Coutinho of the Hawaii County Police has a serial killer of prostitutes to catch and a shortage of leads to pursue. Office Jessie Hokoana of the Honolulu P.D. has an undercover assignment that tests her loyalties and takes her to the brink of death.

When their cases collide in the rainforest of the Big Island, family ties turn deadly, and there may be no *pu'uhonua*—no place of refuge—for anyone.

The Hollow Vessel
An Errol Coutinho/Big Island of Hawaii Mystery
Albert Tucher

Shotgun Honey, an imprint of
Down & Out Books
978-1-946502-93-3

Everyone wants a piece of wealthy young Rhonda Cunningham, which dooms her plan to disappear into the rainforest of the Big Island of Hawaii.

Detective Errol Coutinho needs to find out how her expensive tent ended up on the Kona side of the island.

And is that her blood in it?

It's getting crowded in the rainforest, and the shakeout will be murder…

The Furious Way
Aaron Philip Clark

Shotgun Honey, an imprint of
Down & Out Books
978-1-64396-003-6

Lucy Ramos is out for blood—she needs to kill a man, but she has no clue how. Lucy calls on the help of aged hit-man, Tito Garza, now in his golden years, living a mundane life in San Pedro.

With a backpack full of cash, Lucy persuades Garza to help her murder her mother's killer, ADA Victor Soto. Together, the forgotten hit-man hungry for a comeback and the girl whose life was shattered as a child, set out to kill the man responsible. But killing Victor Soto may prove to be an impossible task...

Once a World
Craig McDonald

Down & Out Books
July 2019
978-1-64396-026-5

Welcome to America, circa 1916-1918, and two of the bloodiest conflicts that starkly defined an era.

Teenage Hector Lassiter, an aspiring author inspired by propaganda and a siren's song of throbbing war drums, lies about his age, mounts a horse, and storms across the Mexican border behind General "Black Jack Pershing" and George S. Patton to bring the terrorist and Revolutionary General Pancho Villa to justice.

Soon, Hector is shipped off to the bloody trenches of France, fighting the so-called "War to End All Wars" where he meets fellow novelists-in-waiting, John Dos Passos and Ernest Hemingway.

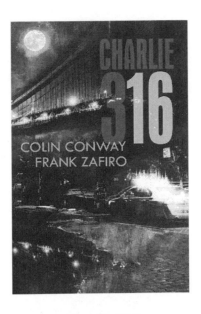

Charlie 316
Colin Conway and Frank Zafiro

Down & Out Books
June 2018
978-1-948235-68-6

A criminal/political thriller surrounding the investigation of an officer-involved shooting.

Surviving an ambush by killing the suspected shooter doesn't guarantee Officer Tyler Garrett safety, especially when the suspect was shot in the back and his gun has disappeared.

Will the department and city hall close ranks and protect Garrett? Or will they step back and allow him to twist in the wind?

Countdown
Matt Phillips

All Due Respect, an imprint of
Down & Out Books
April 2019
978-1-948235-84-6

LaDon and Jessie—two hustlers who make selling primo weed a regular gig—hire a private security detail to move and hold their money. Ex-soldiers Glanson and Echo target the cash—they start a ripoff business. It's the wild, wild west. Except this time, everybody's high.

With their guns and guts, Glanson and Echo don't expect much trouble from a mean son-of-a-gun like LaDon Charles. But that's exactly what they get. In this industry, no matter how much money there is for the taking—and no matter who gets it—there's always somebody counting backwards...to zero.

Man Standing Behind
Pablo D'Stair

All Due Respect, an imprint of
Down & Out Books
May 2019
978-1-64396-035-7

Leaving work on a nondescript evening, Roger is held up at gunpoint when he stops at a cash machine. But robbery isn't on the gunman's mind…Roger is told simply to walk.

The gunman takes him on a macabre odyssey—from city pubs to suburban neighborhoods to isolated homes in the country—and as the night presses on, a seemingly not-so-random body count grows around him.

A man caught in the roils of a mortal circumstance having nothing to do with his own life. Is he a witness, a victim…or something altogether worse?

Made in the USA
Middletown, DE
29 July 2019